Cambridge Critical Workshop

Jeffrey and Lynn Wood

Published by the Press Syndicate of the University of Cambridge
The Pitt Building, Trumpington Street, Cambridge CB2 1RP
40 East 20th Street, New York, NY 10011-4211, USA
10 Stamford Road, Oakleigh, Melbourne, Australia

© Cambridge University Press 1995

First published 1995

Printed in Great Britain by Scotprint, Musselburgh, Scotland

A catalogue record for this book is available from the British Library.

ISBN 0 521 44879 4

Prepared for publication by Paren & Stacey Editorial Consultants
Designed by Geoffrey Wadsley

Acknowledgements

The authors and publishers wish to thank the following for permission to use copyright material:

Faber & Faber Ltd. for Thom Gunn, 'Human Condition' from *The Sense of Movement*; Sylvia Plath, 'Daddy' from *Collected Poems*, ed. Ted Hughes; and T S Eliot, 'Portrait of a Lady' from *Collected Poems 1909-1962*. International Creative Management, Inc. on behalf of the author for extracts from Toni Morrison, *The Bluest Eye*. Copyright © 1970 Toni Morrison. Newspaper Publishing PLC for Zoe Heller, 'Fear and Loathing and Prozac in SoHo', *The Independent on Sunday*, 21.8.94. Rogers, Coleridge and White Ltd. on behalf of the Estate of Angela Carter for an extract from Angela Carter, *The Magic Toyshop*, 1967. Richard Scott Simon Ltd. on behalf of the Estate of Joyce Grenfell for an extract from Joyce Grenfell, 'George Don't Do That' from *Nursery School Sketches*. Copyright © 1977 Joyce Grenfell.

Jenny Hewlett, Lucy Bundy, Sam Udwadia, Michael Cowland, James Lant, Elizabeth Hargrave, Karen Marie Smith, Katherine Hodgson, Polina Bakhnova, Cara de le Mare, Chris Verity, James Baldwin, Lisa Chotia, Alison Scott, Jo Ramsey, Nick Adams and Georgina Leeson for essays written as part of their Advanced Level English courses.

Thanks are also due to the following for permission to reproduce illustrations:

Design and Artists Copyright Society for George Grosz drawing from *Die Räuber*. B T Batsford Ltd. for three drawings, nos 853-5, from Doreen Yarwood, *A Chronology of Western Architecture*. The Bodleian Library, University of Oxford, for Ms Douce 332, fol 58r.

Polina Bakhnova for 'The Kraken', 'A Vision of Hell' and 'Daddy' collage; Vikki Hartley for 'Toyshop'; Tim Elcock for 'Prisoner' and 'Temptation'; Mandy Millbank for 'A Handful of Dust'.

Every effort has been made to trace all the copyright holders, but if any have been inadvertently overlooked the publishers will be pleased to make the necessary arrangements at the first opportunity.

Contents

Preface

We wish to thank students and colleagues, past and present, from the following schools and colleges without whose help this book would never have been written: Ernulf Community School, St Neots; Hitchin Boys' School; Holland Park School, London; Newport (Essex) Free Grammar School; Woodberry Down School, Hackney; The Cambridge Centre for Sixth Form Studies, and Long Road Sixth Form College, Cambridge.

These materials have been developing for some time, prompted, shaped and modified in the light of classroom experience and by what students have found helpful in private study. Without lots of ideas and feedback from students and colleagues, the units in this volume would be less effective than they are. Special thanks are due to B J Frampton, Clare Campbell, Jerry Rowlands, Rex Gibson, Tony Adams, Tom Turner and Julia Long, whose teaching, inspiration, suggestions and advice were invaluable.

Thanks also go to the many students who have written for us over the years and especially to those who have allowed some of their work (not always their best) to be reproduced. The comments of students who have moved on to Higher Education and reflected upon what they found helpful in the various approaches explored here have been enormously instructive. Special thanks, then, to Julian Broughton, Robert Newman, Gareth Owen, Georgina Leeson, Polina Bakhnova, Laura Harrison and Lucy Bundy.

We're indebted, as always, to our editor at CUP, Keith Rose, and to Liz Paren, the free-lance editor, whose incisive and rigorous commentary upon the various drafts of the book helped us to reshape a mountain of material into its present form. Thanks, too, to Jill Rendell for her indefatigable help with word-processing.

Finally we wish to thank the staff and students of Long Road Sixth Form College's peerless Art Department for many of the illustrations. We're indebted to Judith Grant, Val Cornish, Andy Crocker and Neil Payne for their professional assistance.

For the shortcomings, we're to blame.

Jeffrey and Lynn Wood
Cambridge 1994

For Sam

Introduction

Cambridge Critical Workshop is designed to meet the needs of today's typical A, AS and Access English Literature students as they prepare for the Unseen Criticism examination.

It engages students in a variety of ways of responding to unseen material and our hope is that students and their teachers will find all of these techniques useful with a wide range of texts, not just with those we have chosen for this volume.

From the outset the book was planned with the representative A Level English Literature student in mind. There are already some excellent materials available for the handful for whom English Literature is their first subject and who will go on to read for an English degree. But since for the vast majority of students, English Literature is their second or third subject and their goal an average A Level grade, the *Workshop's* assumptions about what students will have read before they start the course and will respond to with enthusiasm and confidence are deliberately modest.

The *Workshop* begins with activities designed to take students gently from the kinds of unseen work many of them will have tackled at Key Stage Four through a series of varied and carefully supported class activities and written assignments towards more demanding tasks where they are given progressively less guidance. We have assumed that groups will be large and heterogeneous and that teachers will wish to use the units in many different ways: for whole class work, for group and pair work and for individual private study. We have given some indication of how long we have found the various activities usually take but of course a great deal depends upon the chemistry of each group. Teachers will find many ways in which the units may be extended or abridged.

Purely for reasons of space, we have decided to concentrate in the present volume upon mainstream prose, poetry and Shakespearean drama, since those areas seem to be the ones with which students initially feel most comfortable.

One of the distinctive features of the *Workshop* is the substantial amount of student writing it contains. In our experience, students learn more readily from one another than from prescription. We haven't found that any of the essays printed here has proved intimidating to students new to this kind of work. In fact what usually happens is that far from being impressed by even the more incisive and original pieces, students are often the toughest of assessors and respond to sample materials with work of their own which is confident, lively and detailed and which challenges both the manner and the substance of what they've seen other students write. Given that our aim is to promote a robust pluralism rather than a tepid uniformity in the English classroom, we're confident that the students' essays we've included in the *Workshop* will be seen by no one as "model answers".

Again, for reasons of space, we have limited the secondary critical material to a single example: an extract from John Carey's provocative study of Donne's "Elegy XIX" (see page 122). It is far from clear what the Core requirement that students show "an awareness of the ways in which readers discover and make different kinds and levels of meaning in texts" can mean in practice with students of average ability. We believe that beginning by giving students the opportunity to respond to what people of their own age have written is the best way of building up their confidence so that towards the end of their courses they can go on to challenge readings "authorised" by a critic's reputation.

The Unseen Question

DEVELOPING A STRATEGY

Writing about an unseen passage is not like writing an essay about a text you have studied in class. The examiner does not expect you to produce an expert, exhaustive reading. What s/he does want to see is that you know the methods a literary critic uses.

When you're faced by an unseen passage, it's worth remembering that whatever the passage, there will be many different aspects of it to examine and comment upon. In an hour or so, no one can talk about everything worth discussing but if you are able to make twenty well-thought-out points, rooted in references to the text, you will have earned enough marks for a good grade.

Always begin by looking carefully at what the question is expecting you to do. Highlight or underline the key words. The examiner may have given you some helpful information, such as when the piece was written and for what purpose.

Next read through the passage three or four times. Once quickly, to get an overview, a general impression of what it is all about, and then two or three times slowly, trying to *hear* the piece in your head as if someone were reading it to you.

If there are parts of the passage you cannot immediately make sense of, concentrate upon the rest. As Eliot said "It is the mark of great poetry that it often communicates before it is fully understood". The same is true of unseen prose and drama. You will often be able to say a great deal about a piece you do not fully understand—you are not being asked to translate the unseen piece into everyday English!

The most important point to remember is not to concentrate too much on just one feature of a passage: the content. The examiner wants to see whether you are aware that *how* the passage is written is as interesting as what it says.

Prose or Poetry?

People often think that prose is not art, in the way that poetry is. Many choose the prose question in the Unseen examination believing that it will be easier to write about than the poem on the opposite page.

Nothing could be further from the truth. The prose you will find on an unseen paper will have been as carefully, as deliberately, as cunningly put together as the poems. And, as with the poems, you must begin by recognising that it is *the way the writer presents her/his material* which you are expected to write about.

Because literary prose at first sight looks like what we write and read every day, writing about a passage of prose is more difficult than writing about poetry, unless you've read lots of literary prose and are aware of how different writers may use the medium. Many people score low marks on the prose passages, because instead of discussing *tone, imagery, rhythm, diction, structure, the writer's intention* and all the things they would talk about if they were examining a poem, they concern themselves just with the story.

Content and Form

At the simplest level, you need to show the examiner that you are aware of these two aspects of the passage.

The *content* is the story, the ideas, the substance, the feelings which the piece of writing conveys to you.

The *form* is the structure, the shape, the construction, the pattern, the medium, the genre in which the writer has decided to present the content. Is it written like a diary entry? a ballad? in blank (unrhymed) verse? in colloquial prose?... A story written as a series of jottings does not have the same impact as it would have were it written in rhyming couplets. An account of a murder described in the peculiar and formal language of a police statement in court would affect you differently if it were whispered to you in the words of a close friend.

When you write about an unseen passage, therefore, be careful not to write just about the *content,* but also to describe what you notice about the *form.*

Tone and Diction

You will also want to write about the *tone of voice* you hear the writer using. Very little literature is written in a flat, mechanical, neutral tone of voice. When you read a piece in the silence of the examination room, try to hear it as if it were being read aloud by an actor.

Often the key to understanding the impact of a piece of writing comes not from the literal meaning of the words but from the tone of voice in which they are spoken. Think about the many different ways in which the words "I really love you" could be said.

Tone is not something you have to guess. If you read a whole piece carefully a few times, you will find that the writer gives clues all the way through about how s/he wants the words to be heard. For example, lots of question marks and pauses suggest someone who's disturbed, confused, muddled:

> What's this? What's this? Is it her fault or mine?
> Who sins most?

Long, steady, flowing sentences suggest a confident, secure, smug even arrogant speaker:

> It took the whole of Creation
> To produce my foot, my each feather:
> Now I hold Creation in my foot

> Or fly up, and revolve it all slowly—
> I kill where I please because it is all mine.

The sorts of words a writer chooses, the *diction,* also affect the way we respond. Someone who describes getting married as "forming a matrimonial alliance" is conveying a very different attitude to marriage from someone who calls it "shacking up together" or the one who uses the cliché "tying the everlasting knot".

On pages 85 and 109 you will find examples of pieces where tone and diction play a particularly powerful part in shaping the way we are expected to read and respond.

Rhythm, Tempo and Texture

The basic difference between poetry and prose is that in most poetry there's a predictable, steady and regular *rhythm.* This rhythm determines which syllables are stressed (have more weight, more emphasis) and which are not. Rhythm can be *regular* or *irregular.* The more regular the rhythm, the more controlled, smooth, polished the piece will be. The more irregular the rhythm, the more disjointed, dramatic, agitated the passage will feel.

For example, in these lines from "Morte D'Arthur" by the nineteenth century poet, Tennyson, there is a pattern of five stresses in each line. Try to tap them out whilst you read the lines. The first line's been set out to show where the stressed syllables come:

> So **all** day **long** the **noise** of **battle rolled**
> Among the mountains by the winter sea,

Until King Arthur's table, man by man,
Had fallen in Lyonesse about their lord,
King Arthur; then, because his wound was deep
The bold Sir Bedivere uplifted him
Sir Bedivere, the last of all his knights,
And bore him to a chapel nigh the field...

Would you describe the rhythm of those lines as regular or irregular? What about the atmosphere, the mood that rhythm creates? What do you notice about the *punctuation* of those lines? How does that affect the way you read it?

In prose too, rhythm can help to determine the mood, the tone, the dramatic impact a piece has. Although it's never as regular as in a poem, the way Dickens uses rhythm here helps to drum home his point:

It contained several large streets all very like one another, and many small streets still more like one another, inhabited by people equally like one another, who all went in and out at the same hours, with the same sound, upon the same pavements, to do the same work, and to whom every day was the same as yesterday and tomorrow, and every year the counterpart of the last and the next...

Tempo is something quite different from rhythm. The tempo of a piece is the speed at which it needs to be read: *fast, moderate* or *slow*. Often the tempo will fluctuate from one extreme to another whilst the rhythm stays the same. At what tempo did you find yourself reading the passage from Tennyson? Was it fast, moderate or slow?

Here are two extracts from Marvell's poem "To His Coy Mistress". The rhythm is in each case the same. But what about the tempo?

We would sit down and think which way
To walk, and pass our long love's day.

But at my back I always hear
Time's winged charriot hurrying near.

In the pieces we look at on pages 42 and 60 the impact of tempo and rhythm are particularly powerful.

Like paint or pottery, words can be smooth or rough in *texture*. In which category would you put each of these words?

frazzled	oozing	mellow	bitchy	anodyne	Jug-Jug
punchy	aspiration	crotchety	hazzard	peace	

Rhythm, tempo and texture working together may suggest serenity:

Sweetest silver speech across
Seven seas of silence
(**Jeni Symes:** *twentieth century*)

irritation:

For God's sake hold your tongue, and let me love
Or chide my palsy, or my gout...
(**John Donne:** *sixteenth century*)

tenderness:

So let us melt, and make no noise,
No tear-floods, nor sigh-tempests move
'Twere profanation of our joys
To tell the laity our love.
(**John Donne:** *sixteenth century*)

or sarcasm:

I say I may be back.
You know what lies are for.
(**Sylvia Plath:** *twentieth century*)

Imagery

Literary writing is often rich with images—pictures in words.
Sometimes the image is simply a *literal* representation of what the
writer wants us to see in our mind's eye. Here Dickens describes Miss
Tox in his novel *Dombey & Son* published in 1848:

She was accustomed to wear odd weedy little flowers in her bonnets
and caps. Strange grasses were sometimes perceived in her hair; and it
was observed by the curious, of all her collars, frills, tuckers, wrist-
bands, and other gossamer articles—indeed of everything she wore
which had two ends to it intended to unite—that the two ends were
never on good terms, and wouldn't quite meet without a struggle.

Often, however, an image is a *figurative* way of describing something:
it is compared to something else with which it has just one thing in
common. Henry James's heroine in *What Maisie Knew* does not look
like a cup. But this is how James, writing in 1897, describes why each
of Maisie's parents wants custody of her after their divorce:

What was clear to any spectator was that the only link binding her to either parent was this lamentable fact of her being a ready vessel for bitterness, a deep little porcelain cup in which biting acids could be mixed.

The imagery that Hopkins uses in his sonnet on page 115 and Lawrence in the opening of "Odour of Chrysanthemums" (see page 24) is particularly important in controlling a response.

Impact

All of these various aspects of a piece of writing contribute to the *impact* it makes on you, the reader. But the full impact will also depend a great deal upon your own imagination, experiences of life and of literature and upon your mood as you read.

Here's an extract from a poem for you to read and respond to. We'll look at how all the features we have been looking at help to shape the way we feel and think about the writing. This is the first stanza of a poem written in 1919 by TS Eliot:

Burbank with a Baedeker:
Bleistein with a Cigar

> Burbank crossed a little bridge
> Descending at a small hotel;
> Princess Volupine arrived,
> They were together and he fell.

The *content* of this is fairly clear. A character called Burbank travelled to a "small hotel" at which someone calling herself "Princess Volupine" arrived. They copulated ("were together") and Burbank "fell"—in other words, he lost his ...? virginity, dignity, reputation, honour, money, manhood or whatever.

The *form* is simple: a stanza (paragraph of poetry) of four lines of verse (called a quatrain) which rhyme abcb (the words at the ends of lines two and four rhyme) and have a four stress-to-a-line rhythm.

To a large extent, the impact this little story has on the reader comes from the mismatch of *content* and *form*. The poet has deliberately chosen an unsuitable form. Would you have chosen to tell such a story in such a way? The sing-song style, nursery-rhyme form is surely inappropriate for a story about a sordid sexual affair? We are more used to it being used for this sort of thing:

"Toads of property" by George Grosz, from *Die Räuber*, Berlin, 1922, © DACS 1995.

> Jack and Jill went up the hill
> To fetch a pail of water
> Jack fell down and broke his crown
> And Jill came tumbling after.

The result of using this *incongruous form* is that we find the piece memorable and, possibly, funny.

But what other details in this piece contribute to the effect it has on the reader? What *tone* would you use to read these lines in? Tender? angry? mocking? frightening? Can you explain why? What about *diction,* the kinds of words the poet has chosen? What do you make of the names of the people involved? Does Burbank sound to you like a large or a small man? Rich or poor? Attractive or unattractive?

Here's an extract from a year thirteen student's essay on this poem:

To me, "Burbank" suggests the words "burly" and "banker": I imagine a certain type of man - fat, wealthy and unhealthy. The texture of the word suggests to me someone clumsy, coarse, or both. Imagining him in that way, I find the images of his crossing a "little" bridge and going to a "small" hotel comical, ridiculous, shabby, sordid, rather pathetic.

And what about his lover, "Princess Volupine"? Is she a real princess? Her name suggests both "voluptuous" (sexy) and "vulpine" (like a fox, crafty). The sinuous texture of the word "volupine" reinforces its feline, predatory feel as you say it. She's a classy prostitute (whether blockhead Burbank realises it or not).

The outcome "and he fell", emphasised by the trite rhyme, is funny because we usually think of a woman "falling" (being seduced by, losing her honour to) an unscrupulous man. Here the roles are reversed, making Burbank look ridiculous.

The rhythm is regular as clockwork; the final stress on "fell" produces part of the comic effect: like watching Burbank fall over on a banana skin. It's difficult not to read the stanza at a moderate walking pace.

The mismatch of content and form, the rhythm and tempo working together here help to convey the scathing, sarcastic tone of the whole thing.

And then there's the title. Burbank's "Baedeker" (a tourist's guidebook) is never mentioned again; we are given the information that he has one simply so that we can see Burbank as a tourist: awkward, naive, easy prey to someone as experienced as "Princess Volupine". The Jewish names "Burbank" and "Bleistein" linked together, especially as

the latter is crudely identified by his "cigar", and the date at which
the poem was written, suggest that a poem with some pretty conventional anti-semitic attitudes is coming, with people presented as
caricatures...

Assignment

Two hours

☐ This poem was written by the Englishman William Blake in 1794.
   Write a study of it, paying particular attention to the ways in which
   content, form, diction, tone, rhythm, tempo and texture contribute
   to the impact it makes on you.

London

I wander through each chartered street
Near where the chartered Thames does flow,
And mark in every face I meet
Marks of weakness, marks of woe.

In every cry of every man,
In every infant's cry of fear,
In every voice, in every ban,
The mind-forged manacles I hear.

manacles: a prisoner's chains

How the chimney-sweeper's cry
Every blackening church appals;
And the hapless soldier's sigh
Runs in blood down palace walls.

hapless: unlucky

But most through midnight streets I hear
How the youthful harlot's curse
Blasts the new-born infant's tear,
And blights with plagues the marriage hearse.

harlot: prostitute

Note: In Blake's time, skinny young boys were sent up chimneys to
brush them clean. Many were injured or suffocated.
   A hearse is the wagon on which a coffin is taken to the graveyard.

Some Things to Ask a Text

Here are some features of the way a piece of literature is written which you may wish to comment upon. Use a highlighter pen to pick out the textual details you will use to illustrate the points you will be developing in your essay.

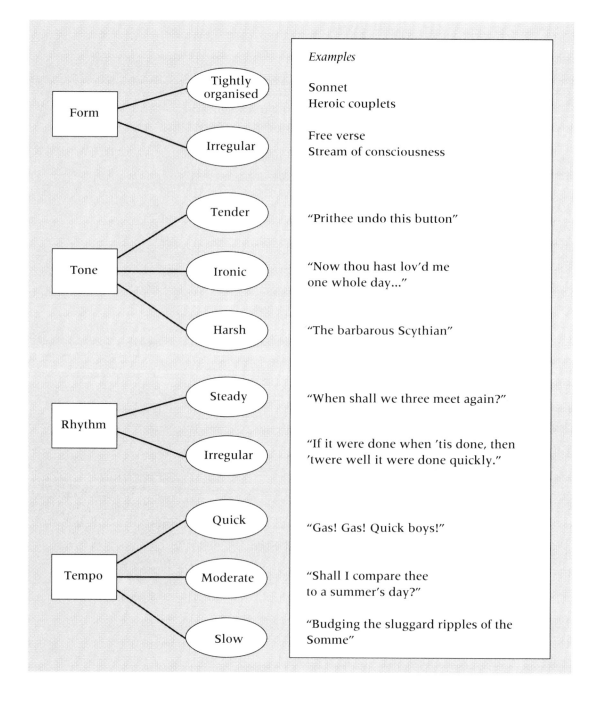

Examples

Form → Tightly organised	Sonnet Heroic couplets
Form → Irregular	Free verse Stream of consciousness
Tone → Tender	"Prithee undo this button"
Tone → Ironic	"Now thou hast lov'd me one whole day..."
Tone → Harsh	"The barbarous Scythian"
Rhythm → Steady	"When shall we three meet again?"
Rhythm → Irregular	"If it were done when 'tis done, then 'twere well it were done quickly."
Tempo → Quick	"Gas! Gas! Quick boys!"
Tempo → Moderate	"Shall I compare thee to a summer's day?"
Tempo → Slow	"Budging the sluggard ripples of the Somme"

Remember that some of these features are likely to *change* in the course of a passage. Sometimes, as in Angelo's soliloquy (see page 105), the tone will shift from moment to moment; the tempo may be leisurely at the beginning and speed up later on. What examiners refer to as the *movement* of a character's thoughts is usually reflected in *changes in the ways s/he expresses them.*

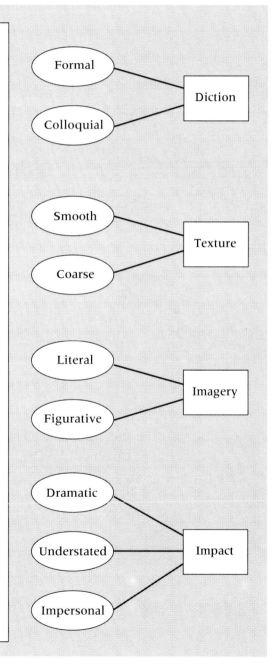

Examples

"Let me not to the marriage of true minds
Admit impediments"

"Daddy, daddy, you bastard,
I'm through."

"that whiter skin of
hers than snow, And smooth,
as monumental alabaster"

"nothing but the composition
of a knave, beggar, coward,
pandar, and the son and heir of a
mongrel bitch"

"And now a gusty shower wraps
The grimy scraps
Of withered leaves about your feet"

"The morning comes
to consciousness"

"Dulce et Decorum Est"
(see page 19)

"The Send-Off"
(see page 19)

What Maisie Knew
(see page 133)

Formal
Colloquial
Diction

Smooth
Coarse
Texture

Literal
Figurative
Imagery

Dramatic
Understated
Impersonal
Impact

What's an English Literature Essay like?

OWEN: DULCE ET DECORUM EST
and THE SEND OFF

It's much easier to learn about essay-writing from reading someone else's work, than from following a list of instructions. This unit therefore shows you parts of an essay which is not a brilliant piece of work, but is typical of the essays successful students write at A level. It goes through some of the critical processes and shows that the student has examined the two poems thoroughly, choosing the details which will help her write her essay by looking closely at the writer's uses of poetic language.

This is the assignment this student was tackling:

Compare and contrast these two poems of Wilfrid Owen in whatever ways you find interesting. What do you think Owen was trying to do in these pieces? How successful do you think he was?

Like most critical assignments, this one suggests you write an essay which will fall into three distinct sections :

Introduction: a sentence or two discussing the circumstances in which Owen was writing and his motives for writing about the war in the way that he did.

Main body: in three parts:
1 a detailed study of "Dulce et Decorum Est";
2 a linking passage discussing the striking differences between the style of "Dulce" and "The Send-Off";
3 a detailed study of "The Send-Off"

Conclusion: a paragraph or two assessing the impact the poems made on you, and exploring how successful the poems are as "moral propaganda".

Here are the poems this student compared in her assignment. Before you read through her essay, you may like to think what you might have written about them:

Dulce Et Decorum Est

Bent double, like old beggars under sacks,
Knock-kneed, coughing like hags, we cursed through sludge,
Till on the haunting flares we turned our backs
And towards our distant rest began to trudge.
Men marched asleep. Many had lost their boots   5
But limped on, blood-shod. All went lame; all blind;
Drunk with fatigue; deaf even to the hoots
Of gas-shells dropping softly behind.

Gas! GAS! Quick, boys!—An ecstasy of fumbling,
Fitting the clumsy helmets just in time;   10
But someone was still yelling out and stumbling
And flound'ring like a man in fire or lime
Dim, through the misty panes and thick green light,
As under a green sea, I saw him drowning.

In all my dreams, before my helpless sight,   15
He plunges at me, guttering, choking, drowning.

If in some smothering dreams you too could pace
Behind the wagon that we flung him in,
And watch the white eyes writhing in his face,
His hanging face, like a devil's sick of sin;   20
If you could hear, at every jolt, the blood
Come gargling from the froth-corrupted lungs,
Obscene as cancer, bitter as the cud
Of vile, incurable sores on innocent tongues, -
My friend, you would not tell with such high zest   25
To children ardent for some desperate glory,
The old Lie: *Dulce et decorum est*
Pro patria mori.

The Send-Off

Down the close, darkening lanes they sang their way
To the siding-shed,
And lined the train with faces grimly gay.

Their breasts were stuck all white with wreath and spray
As men's are, dead.   5

Dull porters watched them, and a casual tramp
Stood staring hard,

Sorry to miss them from the upland camp.
Then, unmoved, signals nodded, and a lamp
Winked to the guard.   10

So secretly, like wrongs hushed-up, they went.
They were not ours:
We never heard to which front these were sent.

Nor there if they yet mock what women meant
Who gave them flowers.   15

Shall they return to beatings of great bells
In wild train-loads?
A few, a few, too few for drums and yells,
May creep back, silent, to still village wells
Up half-known roads.   20

A Student's Response

Owen served in the English army during the first World War. Most people in England had little idea of what a modern battlefield was like: the images of soldiers they saw on recruiting posters and in popular books presented war as a heroic challenge to brave young men: a wonderful chance to win glory and medals by pitting their bravery and endurance against "the Enemy". Men volunteered for the army, boys often lying about their ages, spurred on by slogans such as "Your Country Needs You!"

Owen was shocked and angered by what he saw. Instead of the war being a glorious, heroic struggle between Right and Wrong, "the Enemy" was muddy, waterlogged trenches, cold weather, infection, bad management and weapons of mass destruction like poison gas and tanks.

Owen felt strongly that people, especially the young, had been lied to. He wrote poems intended to shock and tell the British public about the nature of war as it was experienced by himself and his men. He hoped to change the way the public imagined and felt about war.

Owen's poetry's often harsh and brutal, evoking the horror of war, mocking the glamorous pictures used in government propaganda. You could call Owen's poems "moral propaganda".

The first poem begins with a dramatic picture of some soldiers turning their backs on the battle to take some rest. Instead of the media image of a soldier: upright, singing patriotic songs, marching proudly along in his smart uniform, we get this:

> Bent double, like old beggars under sacks,
> Knock-kneed, coughing like hags, we cursed through sludge...

These lines set the mood of the whole poem. The words Owen chooses are deliberately ugly and harsh-sounding:

> Bent double.....beggars
> Knock-kneed, coughing...hags...cursed...sludge

Instead of the expected picture of jolly soldiers marching along, these men are "bent double".... "knock-kneed". The rhythm of these lines is awkward, clumsy, jerky not smooth. The men don't march steadily and smartly, they hobble, stumble. It's not a parade ground they're on but "sludge" they're forcing their tired feet through. The word "sludge" has a sticky texture: as you say it, you can imagine the effort it is to get through the mucky stuff.

These men aren't heroes: well they don't look like heroes or even like men. Owen compares them first to "old beggars" then to broken-down old women - "hags". They're not singing patriotic songs, either, they're cursing.

You couldn't paint a picture of a band of soldiers more different from the ones found in the popular stories of the time than Owen paints here. I can't admire these poor wretches; I can only feel sorry for them.

The opening of this poem appeals to my feelings of pity. But what comes next is horrifying:

> Gas! GAS! Quick boys! - An ecstasy of fumbling
> Fitting the clumsy helmets just in time;

The men were described as "drunk with fatigue" in the first stanza. So sleepy, they didn't notice the mocking "hoots" of gas shells dropping softly behind.

The word "softly" there was sinister. A gas shell doesn't draw attention to itself like a grenade going off but is just as deadly. In the two lines quoted, the officer realises that they are being enveloped by a cloud of deadly gas and gives the order to put on the masks. (The word "Boys" is a touch of pathos in the middle of the horror.) The boy-soldiers' training takes over. They jump into action and get their masks on. The words Owen chooses to describe the operation is another example of the way he can make the rhythm and the texture of the words imitate the action he is describing:

> Gas! GAS! Quick boys! - An ecstasy of fumbling
> Fitting the clumsy helmets just in time;

After the sharp, alert sounds of the command:

> Gas! GAS! Quick boys! -

(I think the second word is in capitals to show it is screamed) come the words describing the panic of the tricky operation of getting helmets on quickly. As you say these words:

> An ecstasy of fumbling
> Fitting the clumsy helmets just in time;

especially if you try to say them quickly, you get tangled up, like a tongue twister. Words such as "ecstasy... fumbling...clumsy... helmets.." are cluttered with clumsy consonants, it's difficult to get your tongue around them. If you read the lines quickly, you get into a sweat. You have to take a deep breath when it's all over.

> . . . . . .just in time;

comes as a great relief.

But then comes the most dramatic touch. The simple word "But". Just as it seemed everything was fine, everyone was safe, comes the horrible realisation that one of the "boys" <u>hasn't</u> managed to complete the clumsy operation "in time".

The description of the soldier's death and what happens to him afterwards is chilling because Owen paints it in such close-up detail.

This essay now explores some details from the rest of the poem and then makes some general points about it: that it uses shock and horror to jolt its readers into realising that "Dulce et Decorum..." is a terrible lie which no one should ever repeat.

The transitional sentence in the body of the essay goes on to say that Owen used a very different poetic technique in "The Send-Off".

In "Dulce" everything's painted in full horror: it is a shocking poem intended to shock people into reconsidering the way war is talked about. In "The Send-Off", Owen uses a more subtle approach. Here, instead of shocking the reader with horror, everything is understated, hinted at, suggested. No harsh sounds, no violent details. The poem is quiet and calm in tone all the way through..."

Now come a few paragraphs looking at the techniques of "The Send-Off" as closely as "Dulce" was studied. Six or so extracts from "The Send-Off" are examined, showing how the diction (choice of words), the tone of voice and the situation of the speaker, the rhythm and the impact of the poem as a whole are so very different from "Dulce". Finally comes a sentence or two commenting on the effectiveness of this very different style of writing.

To round the essay off, there is a paragraph summing up what the student felt Owen hoped to do in his two poems and saying how far she thought he was successful. Did reading either or both of the poems move her? Did she feel able to imagine the situations Owen described, to sympathise with the men?

I think Owen was less concerned to write memorable poems (he said "the poetry does not matter") than to shake up a complacent British public. By using shock-horror tactics as in "Dulce" and a very different, subtle approach as in "The Send-Off" he made sure he got through to his readers by unsettling them - they couldn't just dismiss his writing as "sensationalist" or "clever-clever". I felt sick when I followed the wagon on which the dead boy spewed up blood with every "jolt" of the wheels...

It is a good idea to end with a strong quotation - best of all if it is one you haven't already used. This is how the writer of this essay ends:

I shall never be able to forget that hideous sound Owen evokes so vividly:

> the blood
> Come <u>gargling</u> from the froth-corrupted lungs.

Jenny Hewlett, a year twelve student

Setting the Tone

D H LAWRENCE:
ODOUR OF CHRYSANTHEMUMS

Here's the opening of a short story published by D H Lawrence in 1914. Working individually, read it through quickly and then slowly a few times. When you feel the piece is familiar, underline or highlight what seem to you to be the most interesting details in the passage.

Odour of Chrysanthemums

The small locomotive engine, Number 4, came clanking, stumbling down from Selston with seven full wagons. It appeared round the corner with loud threats of speed, but the colt that it startled from among the gorse, which still flickered indistinctly in the raw afternoon, out-distanced it at a canter. A woman, walking up the railway line to Underwood, drew back into the hedge, held her basket aside, and watched the footplate of the engine advancing. The trucks thumped heavily past, one by one, with slow inevitable movement, as she stood insignificantly trapped between the jolting black wagons and the hedge; then they curved away towards the coppice where the withered oak leaves dropped noiselessly, while the birds, pulling at the scarlet hips beside the track, made off into the dusk that had already crept into the spinney. In the open, the smoke from the engine sank and cleaved to the rough grass. The fields were dreary and forsaken, and in the marshy strip that led to the whimsey, a reedy pit-pond, the fowls had already abandoned their run among the alders, to roost in the tarred fowl-house. The pit-bank loomed up beyond the pond, flames like red sores licking its ashy sides, in the afternoon's stagnant light. Just beyond rose the tapering chimneys and the clumsy black headstocks of Brinsley Colliery. The two wheels were spinning fast up against the sky, and the winding engine rapped out its little spasms. The miners were being turned up.

The engine whistled as it came into the wide bay of railway lines beside the colliery, where rows of trucks stood in harbour.

Miners, single, trailing and in groups, passed like shadows diverging home. At the edge of the ribbed level of sidings squat a low cottage, three steps down from the cinder track. A large bony vine clutched at the house, as if to claw down the tiled roof. Round the bricked yard grew a few wintry primroses. Beyond, the long garden sloped down to a bush-covered brook course. There were some twiggy apple trees, winter-crack trees, and ragged cabbages. Beside the path hung dishevelled pink chrysanthemums, like pink cloths hung on bushes. A woman came stooping out of the felt-covered fowl-house, half-way down the garden. She closed and padlocked the door, then drew herself erect, having brushed some bits from her white apron.

She was a tall woman of imperious mien, handsome, with definite black eyebrows. Her smooth black hair was parted exactly. For a few moments she stood steadily watching the miners as they passed along the railway: then she turned towards the brook course. Her face was calm and set, her mouth was closed with disillusionment. After a moment she called:

"John!" There was no answer. She waited, and then said distinctly:

"Where are you?"

"Here!" replied a child's sulky voice from among the bushes. The woman looked piercingly through the dusk.

"Are you at that brook?" she asked sternly.

For answer the child showed himself before the raspberry-canes that rose like whips. He was a small, sturdy boy of five. He stood quite still, defiantly.

"Oh!" said the mother, conciliated. "I thought you were down at that wet brook—and you remember what I told you—"

The boy did not move or answer.

"Come, come on in," she said more gently, "it's getting dark. There's your grandfather's engine coming down the line!"

The lad advanced slowly, with resentful, taciturn movement. He was dressed in trousers and waistcoat of cloth that was too thick and hard for the size of the garments. They were evidently cut down from a man's clothes.

As they went towards the house he tore at the ragged wisps of chrysanthemums and dropped the petals in handfuls along the path.

"Don't do that—it does look nasty," said his mother. He refrained, and she, suddenly pitiful, broke off a twig with three or four wan flowers and held them against her face. When mother and son reached the yard her hand hesitated, and instead of laying the flower aside, she pushed it in her apron-band. The mother and son stood at the foot of the three steps looking across the bay of lines at the passing home of the miners. The trundle of the small train was imminent. Suddenly the engine loomed past the house and came to a stop opposite the gate.

Thinking/Talking Points

In pairs: thirty minutes

- Without looking back at the passage discuss the details you recall from it and the impression they made on you.
- Now turn to the text. Examine the opening sentences again. What impression of the locomotive does Lawrence give you? How does he do it? You may like to consider features of the language such as *imagery, tone, rhythm* and *diction*.
- What feelings does the picture of the woman presented in the *first* paragraph stir in you? Explain why.
- Pick out a dozen words or phrases from the same paragraph which give it its particular tone (of voice). How would you describe the mood and atmosphere established there?
- Now look at the way Lawrence introduces us to the house. What impression does it make on you? Which images do you feel give the house and its surroundings their special character?
- Read again from "She was a tall woman..." to the end of the extract. We are introduced here to Elizabeth Bates, the person who will be the central character in the story. What is your initial impression of her and her situation?

Assignments

Individual work: two to three hours

Choose one

- ☐ Write a study of this opening of a short story, commenting in detail on the way Lawrence's language creates a particular atmosphere and raises certain expectations.

- ☐ Write a paragraph or two to follow this opening. Try to maintain both the style and the mood which Lawrence has established.
    Then write a detailed commentary on what you have written, explaining what you were trying to do and assessing how successful it was. Discuss the effects created by particular words and phrases in the original and in your continuation.

- ☐ On page 139, you will find a student's response to the first assignment. Read it through carefully and then write a detailed commentary on what he has written, saying what you like about his answer and suggesting ways in which it might be developed or improved. Remember to refer closely to Lawrence's text in your report.

The Writer and the Period

JOHNSON: *from* LIVES OF THE POETS
EMILY BRONTE: *from* WUTHERING HEIGHTS

Writers of different times use quite different styles of poetry and prose. This is something you'll begin to recognise the more widely you read. Like a building, a work of literature is always to some extent a reflection not just of the individual creator's personality but of the manners, the tastes, the expectations and experiences of the period in which it is written.

Do you think the following passage sounds as if it was written recently? Read it through a few times and then see if you can say why.

In acquired knowledge, the superiority must be allowed to Dryden, whose education was more scholastic, and who before he became an author had been allowed more time for study, with better means of information. His mind has a larger range, and he collects his images and illustrations from a more extensive circumference of science. Dryden knew more of man in his general nature, and Pope in his local manners. The notions of Dryden were formed by comprehensive speculation, and those of Pope by minute attention. There is more dignity in the knowledge of Dryden, and more certainty in that of Pope.

That was an extract from an essay written by Samuel Johnson. He is writing about the two most influential poets of the eighteenth century, John Dryden and Alexander Pope. Johnson's "Lives of the Poets" was published in 1781. Johnson is comparing two of his favourite writers and the way he presents his material suggests that Johnson expects his readers to agree with his judgements. Although each poet has distinctive qualities, Johnson feels that, all things carefully considered, Dryden is the greater poet. But this is not to deny that Pope often gives one greater pleasure.

Notice how "reasonable", how sensible Johnson's discussion is. He appeals to his readers' judgements, not to their passions or prejudices. The *tone* is assured but sober and cool, measured, neither dogmatic nor argumentative. Johnson is not going to praise Dryden by rubbishing Pope. That would be unfair, childish and uncritical.

Like the architecture of the time, the style of this writing is carefully

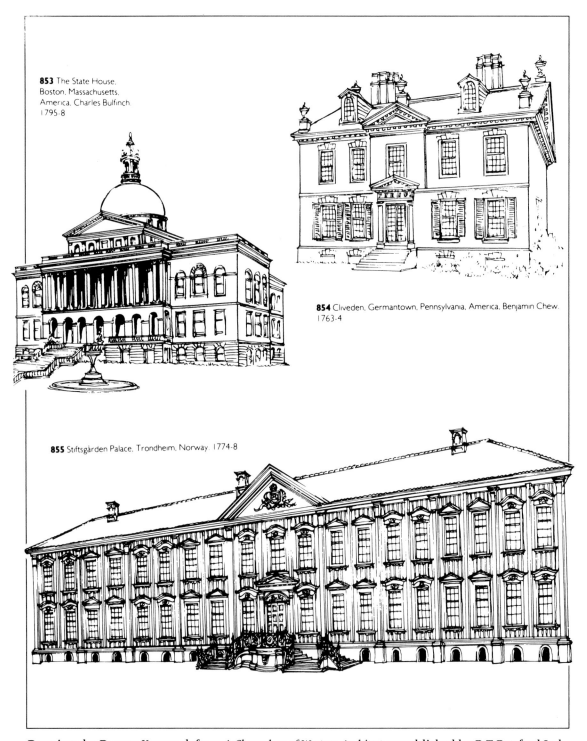

853 The State House, Boston, Massachusetts, America. Charles Bulfinch. 1795-8

854 Cliveden, Germantown, Pennsylvania, America, Benjamin Chew. 1763-4

855 Stiftsgården Palace, Trondheim, Norway. 1774-8

Drawings by Doreen Yarwood, from *A Chronology of Western Architecture* published by B T Batsford Ltd.

balanced, like the writer's judgement. Almost every sentence has an internal balance or symmetry: "on the one hand Dryden is like this, whereas on the other, Pope is like that..."

This deliberate equilibrium, careful balancing of contrasting qualities is called *antithesis.* "If A is red, then B is green. Whilst A may be called experimental, B is more conventional. Although A is an advantage, B may be regarded as a bonus..." The deliberately symmetrical shaping of a piece is characteristic of most eighteenth century art, whether we are looking at a building, a piece of writing or listening to a sonata.

Here's how Johnson's essay continues:

Poetry was not the sole praise of either; for both excelled likewise in prose; but Pope did not borrow his prose from his predecessor. The style of Dryden is capricious and varied, that of Pope is cautious and uniform; Dryden obeys the motions of his own mind, Pope constrains his mind to his own rules of composition. Dryden is sometimes vehement and rapid; Pope is always smooth, uniform, and gentle. Dryden's page is a natural field, rising into inequalities, and diversified by the varied exuberance of abundant vegetation; Pope's is a velvet lawn, shaven by the scythe, and levelled by the roller.

Read through that passage again and look at the way the sentences are structured.

Dr Johnson continues:

Of genius, that power which constitutes a poet; that quality without which judgement is cold and knowledge is inert; that energy which collects, combines, amplifies, and animates; the superiority must, with some hesitation, be allowed to Dryden. It is not to be inferred that of this poetical vigour Pope had only a little, because Dryden had more; for every other writer since Milton must give place to Pope; and even of Dryden it must be said, that if he has brighter paragraphs, he has not better poems. Dryden's performances were always hasty, either excited by some external occasion, or extorted by domestic necessity; he composed without consideration, and published without correction. What his mind could supply at call, or gather in one excursion, was all that he sought, and all that he gave. The dilatory caution of Pope enabled him to condense his sentiments, to multiply his images, and to accumulate all that study might produce, or chance might supply. If the flights of Dryden therefore are higher, Pope continues longer on the wing. If of Dryden's fire the blaze is brighter, of Pope's the heat is more regular and constant. Dryden often surpasses expectation, and Pope never falls below it. Dryden is read with frequent astonishment, and Pope with perpetual delight.

Thinking/Talking Points

- Pick out twenty words which you think are characteristic of Johnson's *diction* in this passage. What words would you use to describe that diction?
- What qualities does Johnson admire in the poetry of (a) Dryden (b) Pope?
- Which do you think is the most memorable sentence in the extract? What makes it so?

Assignment

Two hours

☐ Write a passage of about one hundred words of your own, comparing and contrasting any *city* with any *village* you know, imitating features of Johnson's style. Then write a commentary on what you have produced, describing the ways in which your piece is similar to/different from his. (You may find it interesting to read a student's response to this assignment on page 138.)

To compare with that extract from Johnson's "Lives of the Poets" here's an extract from Emily Bronte's novel *Wuthering Heights*, published in 1847. Read it through a couple of times and then do one of the assignments. You may like to read it aloud, as if you were performing it for a radio audience.

Chapter IX

He entered, vociferating oaths dreadful to hear; and caught me in the act of stowing his son away in the kitchen cupboard. Hareton was impressed with a wholesome terror of encountering either his wild beast's fondness or his madman's rage—for in one he ran a chance of being squeezed and kissed to death, and in the other of being flung into the fire, or dashed against the wall—and the poor thing remained perfectly quiet wherever I chose to put him.

"There, I've found it out at last!" cried Hindley, pulling me back by the skin of my neck, like a dog. "By heaven and hell, you've sworn between you to murder that child! I know how it is, now, that he is always out of my way. But, with the help of Satan, I shall make you swallow the carving knife, Nelly! You needn't laugh; for I've just crammed Kenneth, head-downmost, in the Blackhorse Marsh: and two is the same as one—and I want to kill some of you, I shall have no rest till I do!".

"But I don't like the carving knife, Mr Hindley," I answered, "it has been cutting red herrings—I'd rather be shot if you please."

"You'd rather be damned!" he said, "and so you shall, no law in England can hinder a man from keeping his house decent, and mine's abominable! open your mouth."

He held the knife in his hand, and pushed the point between my teeth: but, for my part, I was never much afraid of his vagaries. I spat it out, and affirmed it tasted detestably—I would not take it on any account.

"Oh!" said he, releasing me, "I see that hideous little villain is not Hareton—I beg your pardon, Nell—if it be, he deserves flaying alive for not running to welcome me, and for screaming as if I were a goblin. Unnatural cub, come hither! I'll teach thee to impose on a good-hearted, deluded father—Now, don't you think the lad would be handsomer cropped? It makes a dog fiercer, and I love something fierce—Get me a scissors—something fierce and trim! Besides, it's infernal affectation—devilish conceit it is—to cherish our ears, we're asses enough without them. Hush, child, hush! well, then, it is my darling! wisht, dry thy eyes—there's a joy; kiss me; what! it won't? kiss me, Hareton! Damn thee, kiss me! By God, as if I would rear such a monster! As sure as I'm living, I'll break the brat's neck."

Assignment

Choose one: two hours

☐ Write a couple of hundred words which might follow on from this extract. Then write a detailed commentary on what you have written. Describe the various features of Emily Bronte's prose style you have tried to imitate and say how successful you think you've been. Quote a few passages from the original and from your continuation in the commentary.

☐ Write an essay comparing and contrasting the passages of Johnson and Emily Bronte in any ways you find interesting. Quote extensively from both pieces and examine not only the subjects they write about but *the way they present them.* You may wish to comment on such features as the *diction, tone, imagery, rhythm* and the *structure* of their pieces as well as their very different subject matter.

Establishing a Theme

You may come across a question on an Unseen paper similar to this: *Examine the way the writer has presented her/his theme in the following passage...*

If somebody asked you what Shakespeare's play *Antony and Cleopatra* was about, you could give them different sorts of answers. Assuming you knew the play, your answer to that question might begin something like this: "It's the story of Antony, a world-famous, middle-aged Roman war-hero who's fallen in love with the Egyptian queen, Cleopatra, the most fascinating woman of all time and how he..." Or like this: "It's a study of a conflict of loyalties. About whether you should do your duty to your country or do your duty to yourself". Or like this: "It's a play about the nature of reality: about whether temporary worldly triumphs are worth anything compared to the eternal spirituality of love".

The first answer leads to a retelling of the story. The other two are concerned with ideas, with what critics call *themes*. Some works of literature are particularly interesting for the ideas, or themes, they explore. The plot develops as it does, the characters are presented as they are, because the author is using them to explore certain issues, principles or attitudes.

Novels which are particularly interested in exploring ideas about society are sometimes described as "didactic" or "satirical". "Didactic" means instructive. "Satirical" means making something ridiculous in order to make people see how absurd/unjust it is. Two examples of novels which are didactic and satirical are Swift's *Gulliver's Travels* and Margaret Atwood's *The Handmaid's Tale*. They can be enjoyed because they explore some very powerful ideas in dramatic ways, not because the characters or plots are convincingly realistic.

Here is the opening of Dickens's novel *Hard Times,* published in 1854.

Book the First
Chapter One—The One Thing Needful

"Now, what I want is, Facts. Teach these boys and girls nothing but Facts. Facts alone are wanted in life. Plant nothing else, and root out everything else. You can only form the minds of reasoning animals upon Facts: nothing else will ever be of any service to them. This is the principle on which I bring up my own children, and this is the principle on which I bring up these children. Stick to the Facts, Sir!"

The scene was a plain, bare, monotonous vault of a schoolroom, and the speaker's square forefinger emphasized his observations by underscoring every sentence with a line on the schoolmaster's sleeve. The emphasis was helped by the speaker's square wall of a forehead, which had his eyebrows for its base, while his eyes found commodious cellarage in two dark caves, overshadowed by the wall. The emphasis was helped by the speaker's mouth, which was wide, thin, and hard set. The emphasis was helped by the speaker's voice which was inflexible, dry, and dictatorial. The emphasis was helped by the speaker's hair, which bristled on the skirts of his bald head, a plantation of firs to keep the wind from its shining surface, all covered with knobs, like the crust of a plum pie, as if the head had scarcely warehouse-room for the hard facts stored inside. The speaker's obstinate carriage, square coat, square legs, square shoulders—nay, his very neckcloth, trained to take him by the throat with an unaccommodating grasp, like a stubborn fact, as it was—all helped the emphasis.

"In this life, we want nothing but Facts, Sir; nothing but Facts!"

The speaker, and the schoolmaster, and the third grown person present, all backed a little, and swept with their eyes the inclined plane of little vessels then and there arranged in order, ready to have imperial gallons of facts poured into them until they were full to the brim.

Thinking/Talking Points

Small groups: one hour

- Dickens's vigorous prose is good for performing or reading aloud. Before you start analysing the extract, experiment with different ways of performing it.
- Have a go at drawing a cartoon of the speaker in this passage, based on the information Dickens gives us.

- The speaker in this passage is talking about his idea of education. Think up some definitions of the word. Do you think "education" is the same as "training" or "conditioning"? What do you think makes an education "good" or "bad"?
- What effect does Dickens's repetition of certain words have on you and the way you respond to the situation he presents?
- "Now, what I want is, Facts" does not tell us very much. Describe more fully in your own words what you think the speaker feels a good education consists of.
- Does Dickens present the speaker in such a way that we cannot choose how we feel about him? Which words and phrases shape the way you respond to what the speaker says?
- On the basis of this piece, what do you think the theme of Dickens's novel might be? Devise a simple story-line for it.
- Has any of your education been like the one recommended by Dickens's speaker? What have been the best/worst things about your own education? Who has been responsible for teaching you most?
- If you could plan the way your children would spend their time between the ages of five and ten, what kind of environment and what sort of activities would you choose to give them?

Assignments

Choose one: one hour

☐ Rewrite Dickens's piece, making the speaker the spokesperson for your ideas. Make his/her words reflect what you want your children to experience as they develop.

☐ Paying close attention to the way he uses *imagery, diction* and *rhythm,* examine how Dickens introduces his theme in the opening chapter of *Hard Times.*

☐ Rewrite this episode as if you were one of the children being talked about. Use some of the material Dickens has provided but develop in your own way the private thoughts of one of the boys or girls.

   Then write a brief commentary on what you have written, comparing it with the original. In what respects are the two passages similar/different?

Stream of Consciousness

JAMES JOYCE: *from* ULYSSES

Sitting here at the word-processor, I'm aware of many things. I think most of my thoughts are concentrated on what I'm trying to say to you. That alone involves many things: what I feel's important or interesting for a literature student; how best to convey it so you'll understand and enjoy what you read...

Every time I click the keys, I know that choosing a clumsy word or phrase or the wrong tone of voice will confuse or annoy somebody. I'm also very aware that working as fast as I do, my two-finger approach to the keyboard is throwing up hundreds of errors as I gallop along, all of which will have to be scrupulously, time-consumingly corrected later. Groan! I'm cross again I never bothered to learn to touch-type. Is it too late to start now...? Does anyone sell a package?

Even while I try to concentrate on this simple writing task, I realise that I am aware of hundreds of other things too : bits of music (what's that playing downstairs? Where have I heard it before...?) Two of my sons squabbling about breakfast—should I break off? get up and sort that out?—Lynn's talking to someone at the door (don't recognise the voice, wonder if it's that man selling dusters again). And still there's that nagging pain in my upper left molar which needs a filling, (must remember to make another appointment, can't make the one booked for Tuesday as there's a meeting after College : damn!)... the glare of the daylight bulb on the screen, the itching of my scalp, the chill on my back (the front door's open and it's trying to snow outside : I wish that caller would go...). The need to get this piece finished before we have to go out for lunch with some friends, the way that will be difficult—one of them's just lost his mother. The fact that we must get back by six if we're to be here for an important phone call...

That was to illustrate that usually when someone writes a novel they present an artificial, stylised, limited representation of "real life". At any and every moment of our waking day we are conscious, half-conscious, vaguely conscious, preoccupied with hundreds of things simultaneously, not with just one thought, sensation or feeling.

Traditional narrative form is highly selective. Quite artificial.

So for example, when Jane Austen, in the first chapter of her novel *Pride and Prejudice*, neatly sums up Mrs Bennet like this:

She was a woman of mean understanding, little information and uncertain temper. When she was discontented she fancied herself nervous. The business of her life was to get her daughters married; its solace was visiting and news.

the writer is announcing to us that Mrs Bennet is a character in a novel, not somebody in real life. Even the simplest person we meet has much more going on in her head than Jane Austen will tell us about Mrs Bennet. Jane Austen's character has no digestive system, for example, no memories of how her parents treated her when she was a child or feelings about rainbows. Mrs Bennet has no *personality* beyond the formula Jane Austen has given us at the outset. Fiction is a highly *selective* and stylised way of presenting *reality*.

Assignment

Forty minutes

☐ Close your eyes for a couple of minutes and try to identify all the different things which you're conscious of. Sensations: hearing, smelling, physical feelings. Thoughts: what's the point of this exercise? Do I understand what the writer's getting at? When's my next assignment due in...? Feelings. Memories of what happened last night, last week, last year. Anticipations about what's going to be happening tonight, tomorrow, next June...

Then try writing down (or speaking into a tape recorder) all the things that passed through your mind in just those two minutes. Do it as quickly but as fully as you can. Give yourself half an hour to do the job.

Look at/listen to what you produced. How well did you capture those two minutes' experience? What was tricky about getting it all down? What happened to the ways you used words, sentences, tenses, structures and grammar? What do you think was gained and lost by trying to capture your experience so fully?

In 1922 the Irish writer James Joyce published a novel called *Ulysses*. It's about seven hundred pages long and tries to chart the mental experiences of two characters on a single day. Joyce was the first writer to attempt to write in this "stream of consciousness" style on such an ambitious scale. Here's an extract from the novel. One of the central characters, Leopold Bloom, is on his way to the funeral of a friend, Paddy Dignam:

Martin Cunningham, first, poked his silkhatted head into the creaking carriage and, entering deftly, seated himself. Mr Power stepped in after him, curving his height with care.

—Come on, Simon.

—After you, Mr Bloom said.

Mr Dedalus covered himself quickly and got in, saying:

—Yes, yes.

—Are we all here now? Martin Cunningham asked. Come along, Bloom.

Mr Bloom entered and sat in the vacant place. He pulled the door to after him and slammed it tight till it shut tight. He passed an arm through the armstrap and looked seriously from the open carriage window at the lowered blinds of the avenue. One dragged aside: an old woman peeping. Nose white flattened against the pane. Thanking her stars she was passed over. Extraordinary the interest they take in a corpse. Glad to see us go we give them such trouble coming. Job seems to suit them. Huggermugger in corners. Slop about in slipper-slappers for fear he'd wake. Then getting it ready. Laying it out. Molly and Mrs Fleming making the bed. Pull it more to your side. Our wind-ingsheet. Never know who will touch you dead. Wash and shampoo. I believe they clip the nails and the hair. Keep a bit in an envelope. Grow all the same after. Unclean job.

All waited. Nothing was said. Stowing in the wreaths probably. I am sitting on something hard. Ah, that soap in my hip pocket. Better shift it out of that. Wait for an opportunity.

All waited. Then wheels were heard from in front turning: then nearer: then horses' hoofs. A jolt. Their carriage began to move, creaking and swaying. Other hoofs and creaking wheels started behind. The blinds of the avenue passed and number nine with its craped knocker, door ajar. At walking pace.

They waited still, their knees jogging, till they had turned and were passing along the tramtracks. Tritonville Road. Quicker. The wheels rattled rolling over the cobbled causeway and the crazy glasses shook rattling in the doorframes.

—What way is he taking us? Mr Power asked through both windows.

—Irishtown, Martin Cunningham said. Ringsend. Brunswick Street.

Mr Dedalus nodded, looking out.

—That's a fine old custom, he said. I am glad to see it has not died out.

All watched awhile through their windows caps and hats lifted by passers. Respect. The carriage swerved from the tramtrack to the smoother road past Watery Lane. Mr Bloom at gaze saw a lithe young man, clad in mourning, a wide hat.

– There's a friend of yours gone by, Dedalus, he said.

– Who is that?

– Your son and heir.

—Where is he? Mr Dedalus said, stretching over across.

The carriage, passing the open drains and mounds of ripped up roadway before the tenement houses, lurched round the corner and, swerving back to the tramtrack, rolled on noisily with chattering wheels. Mr Dedalus fell back, saying:

—Was that Mulligan cad with him? His *fidus Achates!*

—No, Mr Bloom said. He was alone.

—Down with his aunt Sally, I suppose, Mr Dedalus said, the Goulding faction, the drunken little costdrawer and Crissie, papa's little lump of dung, the wise child that knows her own father.

Mr Bloom smiled joylessly on Ringsend road. Wallace Bros the bottleworks. Dodder bridge.

Richie Goulding and the legal bag. Goulding, Collis and Ward he calls the firm. His jokes are getting a bit damp. Great card he was. Waltzing in Stamer Street with Ignatius Gallaher on a Sunday morning, the landlady's two hats pinned on his head. Out on the rampage all night. Beginning to tell on him now: that backache of his, I fear. Wife ironing his back. Thinks he'll cure it with pills. All breadcrumbs they are. About six hundred per cent profit.

—He's in with a lowdown crowd, Mr Dedalus snarled. That Mulligan is a contaminated bloody doubledyed ruffian by all accounts. His name stinks all over Dublin. But with the help of God and His blessed mother I'll make it my business to write a letter one of those days to his mother or his aunt or whatever she is that will open her eye as wide as a gate. I'll tickle his catastrophe, believe you me.

He cried above the clatter of the wheels.

—I won't have her bastard of a nephew ruin my son. A counterjumper's son. Selling tapes in my cousin, Peter Paul M'Swiney's. Not likely.

He ceased. Mr Bloom glanced from his angry moustache to Mr Power's mild face and Martin Cunningham's eyes and beard, gravely shaking. Noisy selfwilled man. Full of his son. He is right. Something to hand on. If little Rudy had lived. See him grow up. Hear his voice in the house. Walking beside Molly in an Eton suit. My son. Me in his eyes. Strange feeling it would be. From me. Just a chance. Must have been that morning in Raymond Terrace she was at the window, watching the two dogs at it by the wall of the cease to do evil. And the sergeant grinning up. She had that cream gown on with the rip she never stitched. Give us a touch, Poldy. God, I'm dying for it. How life begins.

Got big then. Had to refuse the Greystones concert. My son inside her. I could have helped him on in life. I could. Make him independent. Learn German too.

—Are we late? Mr Power asked.

—Ten minutes, Martin Cunningham said, looking at his watch.

Molly. Milly. Same thing watered down. Her tomboy oaths. O
jumping Jupiter! Ye gods and little fishes! Still, she's a dear girl. Soon
be a woman. Mullingar. Dearest Papli. Young student. Yes, yes: a
woman too. Life. Life.

Thinking/Talking Points

In small groups

- Without looking back at the text jot down from memory as many
  details as you can. Do not bother too much with the order. Compare
  what you remembered with what other people recalled.
- Now listen to somebody reading the extract again.
- Discuss the impression the passage gives each of you of Leopold
  Bloom. Pick out the details which give you that impression.
- What seems to you to be the gains/losses of using this *stream of
  consciousness* style? Which passages do you think are most/least effective? See if you can explain why.

Assignments

Choose one: two hours

☐ Write a further few paragraphs which you feel could follow on from
  this extract from Joyce's novel. Try to maintain the *style* of the original and the *tone* of the narrator.
  Then write a detailed commentary on what you have written
  describing the features of Joyce's piece you were trying to imitate
  and assessing your degree of success.

☐ Produce a collage or story-board suggested by Joyce's extract.

☐ Write an essay in which you examine the impression Joyce gives us
  of Leopold Bloom in the passage from *Ulysses*. Refer closely to the
  particular techniques Joyce uses to create that impression.

Lewis Carroll

from THROUGH THE LOOKING GLASS AND WHAT ALICE FOUND THERE

"You seem very clever at explaining words, Sir," said Alice. "Would you kindly tell me the meaning of the poem called "Jabberwocky"?"

"Let's hear it," said Humpty Dumpty. "I can explain all the poems that ever were invented—and a good many that haven't been invented just yet."

This sounded very hopeful, so Alice repeated the first verse:

> *"Twas brillig, and the slithy toves*
> *Did gyre and gimble in the wabe:*
> *All mimsy were the borogoves,*
> *And the mome raths outgrabe."*

"That's enough to begin with," Humpty Dumpty interrupted: "there are plenty of hard words there. *'Brillig'* means four o'clock in the afternoon—the time when you begin *broiling* things for dinner."

"That'll do very well," said Alice : "and *'slithy'*?"

"Well, *'slithy'* means 'lithe and slimy'. 'Lithe' is the same as 'active'. You see it's like a portmanteau*—there are two meanings packed up into one word."

"I see it now," Alice remarked thoughtfully: "and what are *'toves'*?"

"Well, *'toves'* are something like badgers—they're something like lizards—and they're something like corkscrews."

"They must be very curious-looking creatures."

"They are that," said Humpty-Dumpty: "and also they make their nests under sun-dials—also they live on cheese."

"And what's to *'gyre'* and to *'gimble'*?"

"To *'gyre'* is to go round and round like a gyroscope. To *'gimble'* is to make holes like a gimblet."

"And *'the wabe'* is the grass-plot round a sundial, I suppose?" said Alice, surprised at her own ingenuity.

"Of course it is. It's called *'wabe'* you know, because it goes a long way before it, and a long way behind it – ."

"And a long way beyond it on each side," Alice added.

"Exactly so. Well then, *'mimsy'* is...."

Note: a **portmanteau** is what we'd call a hold-all, a large collapsable bag made of canvas or some other heavy material.

Assignment

Ninety minutes

☐ In this conversation, Humpty Dumpty has explained to Alice the meaning of half the quatrain of "Jabberwocky" she has asked him about. Imitating Lewis Carroll's style, see if you can provide the rest of his explanation.

Then write a commentary on what you have produced, describing the various features of the original which you've tried to copy and say how successful you think you've been.

from SPRING DAY

Preliminary Assignment

Individual work: one hour

A busy city street; you are Christmas shopping or hunting for some new clothes or CDs for yourself.

Picture dozens of people streaming past. Look at the outfits, the different noses, eyes, profiles, hair styles, expressions. What faces can you imagine?

How do your feet feel, pounding the pavement? How's your back?

What's the weather doing? Is it getting dark yet?

What sounds can you hear?

What smells do your nostrils pick up?

Imagine the bits of things you glimpse and then lose sight of as you try to cross the road, thronged with snarling, smelly traffic ...

How does it feel, being jostled and shoved, as you push your way through a big store, looking for the escalator? How do you know it's the perfume department? the toy shop? gardening?

Imagine the snatches of conversation in so many different voices you hear as you make for the exit.

☐ Write a poem, or a piece of prose of about two hundred words, in which you try to convey to the reader the atmosphere of the scene you have imagined.

Here is Amy Lowell's impression of such a scene in 1916 from her prose-poem "Spring Day":

Midday and Afternoon

Swirl of crowded streets. Shock and recoil of traffic. The stock-still brick facade of an old church, against which the waves of people lurch and withdraw. Flare of sunshine down side-streets. Eddies of light in the windows of chemists' shops, with their blue, gold, purple jars, darting colours far into the crowd. Loud bangs and tremors, murmurings out of high windows, whirling of machine belts, blurring of horses and motors. A quick spin and shudder of brakes on an electric car, and the jar of a church bell knocking against the metal blue of the sky. I am a piece of the town, a bit of blown dust, thrust along with the crowd. Proud to feel the pavement under me, reeling with feet. Feet tripping, skipping, lagging, dragging, plodding doggedly, or springing up and advancing on firm elastic insteps. A boy is selling papers, I smell them clean and new from the press. They are fresh like the air, and pungent as tulips and narcissus.

The blue sky pales to lemon, and great tongues of gold blind the shop-windows putting out their contents in a flood of flame.

Thinking/Talking Points

- Discuss how Amy Lowell makes this sound so rich, so full of movement and colour.

  Describe what each of these phrases make you see, hear, feel or smell.

  > Swirl of crowded streets;
  > the jar of a church bell knocking against the metal blue of the sky;

  How has the poet packed so much information into each of these phrases?

  Pick out half a dozen other phrases you particularly enjoy and describe how they make their impact on you.

- Which details in this prose-poem tell us it was written many years ago? For each of these details, suggest a phrase of your own to describe a spring day in a modern city you know well.

Second Assignment

Individual work: one hour

Choose one

☐ Write an appreciation of Amy Lowell's piece. What do you think she is trying to do? What is distinctive about the way she does it? Select and comment upon eight or nine details which impress you and describe how they achieve their effect.

☐ Imagine a city scene similar to the one which Amy Lowell described but at a different time of year or at a different time of day or at a different period of history. Write a piece of your own in a similar style with one of these titles:

Early Morning	Rush Hour	Sunday
Night Time	Winter Day	August

Third Assignment

In pairs: one hour

☐ On page 143 you will find some students' responses to Amy Lowell's piece. Read each of them through a couple of times and then discuss those points you find interesting or think need developing or could be better expressed. Comment upon the way each student has set about organising her/his critical response to the passage.

Research Assignment

In 1917, the American poet T S Eliot published a poem called "Preludes". It uses vivid images to convey an impression of a modern city. Make a comparative study of Eliot's poem and Amy Lowell's piece.

What stylistic features do they have in common? Do you feel they convey similar or different feelings about the places they evoke? Say why, quoting extensively from both works.

Joyce Grenfell

from SING-SONG TIME

Assignments

Ninety minutes: choose one

☐ Here is the opening of a short story. Read it through carefully a couple of times, noting what is distinctive about its *tone*, *diction*, and *style*. Then write three or four further paragraphs continuing the story in what you think would be a suitable way.

Write a commentary on what you have written, describing the features of the original you have tried to imitate and saying how successful you feel you've been. Quote from the original and from your imitation in your essay.

☐ On page 147 you will find a student's response to the question above. Read it through carefully and then write a detailed commentary on how well you feel she has carried out the assignment. In what respects do you think her response could be improved?

Sing-Song Time

Children, we've had our run around the classroom, and now it's time to start our day's work. We're going to have a sing-song together, and Miss Boulting is going to play for us, so come and settle down over here, please.

Kenny, why haven't you taken your coat off?

No, it isn't time to go home yet, Kenny!

You've only just come.

You'd rather go home? Bad luck.

No, you can't go, not quite yet.

Kenny, you've only been here about ten minutes. Come and sit on the floor next to Susan. You like Susan.

No, Susan, I don't think he wants to sit on your lap.

No, I thought he didn't.

Kenny! We don't want to see your tongue, thank you.

No, not even a little bit of it. Put it back, please.

All of it.

And give your jacket to Caroline, I'm sure she'll hang it up for you.

Thank you, Caroline.

Who is that whistling?

Sidney, you know we never whistle indoors.

You can whistle in the garden, but never whistle indoors.

Yes, I know you have just whistled indoors, but don't do it any more.

And don't punch Jacqueline.

I'm sure she didn't say she liked you punching her, did you Jacqueline?

Well, I don't think it's a good idea, so we won't have any more punching.

He is rather a disruptive element in our midst, Miss Boulting, but he does try to belong more than he used to, so we are encouraged, bless his heart.

Let's be *kind* to each other today, shall we? We are going to learn some more of the Drum Marching Song we began yesterday.

Who remembers how it starts?

No, David, it doesn't begin "Twinkle, Twinkle Little Star". That's another song.

Yes, I know you know it, but we aren't going to sing it now.

No. Not today.

And not tomorrow.

I don't know when.

We are going to sing our Drum Marching Song now.

Edgar and Neville, why are you standing on those chairs?

You can see into the fish-tank perfectly well from the floor. Get down please.

No, Neville, you can't hold a fish in your hand.

Because fishes don't like being held in people's hands. They don't like coming out of the water, you see. Their home is in the water.

Well, they do have to come out of the water when we eat them, but these aren't *eating* fishes. These are *friend* fishes. It's Phyllis and Fred. We wouldn't want to eat Phyllis and Fred.

No, Sidney, you wouldn't.

I don't think they'd be better than sausages.

Scott Fitzgerald

from THE GREAT GATSBY

Here's a passage from a novel published in 1925 in which the central character's world is described through the eyes and consciousness of one of his neighbours. Working in pairs, first read it through silently a couple of times then read it aloud, taking a paragraph each in turn.

There was music from my neighbour's house through the summer nights. In his blue gardens men and girls came and went like moths among the whisperings and the champagne and the stars. At high tide in the afternoon I watched his guests diving from the tower of his raft, or taking the sun on the hot sand of his beach while his two motor-boats slit the waters of the Sound, drawing aquaplanes over cataracts of foam. On week-ends his Rolls-Royce became an omnibus, bearing parties to and from the city between nine in the morning and long past midnight, while his station wagon scampered like a brisk yellow bug to meet all trains. And on Mondays eight servants, including an extra gardener, toiled all day with mops and scrubbing-brushes and hammers and garden-shears, repairing the ravages of the night before.

Every Friday five crates of oranges and lemons arrived from a fruiterer in New York—every Monday these same oranges and lemons left his back door in a pyramid of pulpless halves. There was a machine in the kitchen which could extract the juice of two hundred oranges in half an hour if a little button was pressed two hundred times by a butler's thumb.

At least once a fortnight a corps of caterers came down with several hundred feet of canvas and enough coloured lights to make a Christmas tree of Gatsby's enormous garden. On buffet tables, garnished with glistening hors-d'oeuvre, spiced baked hams crowded against salads of harlequin designs and pastry pigs and turkeys bewitched to a dark gold. In the main hall a bar with a real brass rail was set up, and stocked with gins and liquors and with cordials so long forgotten that most of his female guests were too young to know one from another.

By seven o'clock the orchestra has arrived, no thin five-piece affair, but a whole pitful of oboes and trombones and saxophones and viols and cornets and piccolos, and low and high drums. The last swimmers have come in from the beach now and are dressing upstairs; the cars from New York are parked five deep in the drive, and already the halls and salons and verandas are gaudy with primary colours, and hair bobbed in strange new ways, and shawls beyond the dreams of Castile. The bar is in full swing, and floating rounds of cocktails permeate the garden outside, until the air is alive with chatter and laughter, and casual innuendo and introductions forgotten on the spot, and enthusiastic meetings between women who never knew each other's names.

The lights grow brighter as the earth lurches away from the sun, and now the orchestra is playing yellow cocktail music, and the opera of voices pitches a key higher. Laughter is easier minute by minute, spilled with prodigality, tipped out at a cheerful word. The groups change more swiftly, swell with new arrivals, dissolve and form in the same breath; already there are wanderers, confident girls who weave here and there among the stouter and more stable, become for a sharp, joyous moment the centre of a group, and then, excited with triumph, glide on through the sea-change of faces and voices and colour under the constantly changing light.

Thinking/Talking Points

- Put the passage to one side. Discuss the details which you remember. What impression did each of those details make upon you?
- Try to agree on some words which might be picked from this list to describe one of Gatsby's parties.

rowdy   exclusive   vulgar   cheap   fun   magical   raucous
empty   vivacious   meaningless   dream-like   ugly
magnificent   wicked   exotic   indulgent   glamorous
superficial   ostentatious   sinister   tedious   exciting
sumptuous   grand   dreary   exuberant   regal   showy
bright   garish   vibrant   extravagant   gross   crazy
snooty   elegant   naff   mysterious   enticing   tacky
disgusting   enthralling   romantic...

For each word you select, find a detail in the text which supports choosing it.

- Now read through the passage again. Just over half way through the extract, Fitzgerald changes from the past to the present tense. Discuss the effect the change makes and why you think Fitzgerald may have chosen to shape this piece in this way.
- Choose a dozen images from the passage and arrange them to make

a poem which you feel captures the essence of the scene.

Compare your prose-poem with those made up by other pairs.

Assignments

Choose one: ninety minutes

☐ Write a critical examination of this piece, looking at the various devices the writer uses to create his impression of Gatsby's world. You may wish to consider such things as *point of view, imagery, rhythm, diction, tone* and the *shape of the piece*.

  Use plenty of brief quotations in your study.

☐ Using the information from the passage, imagine that you were one of the guests. Write a diary entry or a letter to a friend or relative about your first experience of one of Gatsby's parties.

☐ Compare the extract above with the following representation of the scene through the eyes of a very different kind of observer. It was written by a year twelve student, Lucy Bundy. To what extent do you feel Lucy has significantly changed the experience Fitzgerald's observer described?

  Compare and contrast the style of her writing with Fitzgerald's in any ways you find interesting. Quote freely from both passages in your essay.

Gatsby's Party, seen from the Eyes of a Cherub in his Garden

I remember those sun-drenched summer days of long ago, when I would lie alone in the garden, high above the rest of the world on my pedestal in the fountain, baking in the heat.

Comfortably numb, seduced by the sunshine, afternoon would melt lazily into evening, and I would relax quietly as the weather cooled until nightime fell softly onto my naked, marble shoulders, encompassing me completely, the stars winking as if to kiss me goodnight.

Yes, that's how it used to be, those good old days. How much I took for granted then, my peace, solitude, tranquillity.

All gone now. Gone. Because of him. Gatsby. He moved in here a couple of years ago, and with him came trouble. Guests and visitors at all times, wild noisy parties going on all night. Disgusting, wasteful behaviour.

From my seat way above the lawns and flowerbeds, I see everything, the shocking goings on of the shameless young hussies, hordes of which come and go from this house, their drunken, rowdy man friends chasing after them, relentlessly pursuing them, wooing them with expensive gifts. Oh, yes, I've seen it all, and in a short time I shall see more, for here come the servants, carrying the starched, white linen tablecloths which they will stretch over the huge, long tables, already erected, standing to attention in the huge marquee.

Old Willoughby the butler busies himself by pushing a duster over the brass rim of the bar, putting that final sparkle on the rail around the dance floor. Everything is ready and an air of anticipation settles over the garden. The band start playing softly, and the guests start to arrive in their clusters.

The soft, satisfying crunch of gravel can be heard as the wheels of a motor car roll up the driveway bringing inside it expectant, excited passengers, dressed up to the nines and ready to dance the night away.

The car door opens and out steps a portly, middle aged man, some silly peach of a girl hanging on his arm, her face sparkling with sheer exuberance, her dress winking with sequins and tassels. With heads turning and eyes flickering, they enter the garden, monitoring exactly who is here and what they are doing.

The separate groups mingle and merge together as one, break up and re-emerge as new constellations, different formations, the movement never stops, the throng swarms and swirls, the people weave in and out, round and about one another. It tires me just to watch them. I cannot help but feel a surge of anger and sadness as I observe these silly, superficial beings, who see no further than their next glass of champagne, look no further than the outfit of the person next to them.

Fools.

They don't give a thought to the sweet, green grass which they stand upon, nor the rich, dark soil from which it grows. Never do they look to the sky and see the pale, pregnant moon staring down, shining in the dark molasses of the firmament.

They do not hear the crickets singing in the trees and bushes, they do not stop to enjoy the exquisite shape and form of the petals that tremble and glisten, weighted with the evening dew.

I see these people and pain creeps into my heart. They are trespassers in my garden, intruders into my soul and space. I turn my head to the darkness and I weep. I weep for the darkness of a man's heart, for the loss of innocence and for the loss of a dear, sweet life I used to know.

Alfred, Lord Tennyson

THE KRAKEN

Preparing a Performance

Thirty minutes

Working in pairs or small groups, read the following poem aloud a few times. Experiment with different tones of voice and different tempos until you feel you have caught the mood you feel Tennyson was trying to convey to his listeners. Think particularly about where to pause for dramatic effect and where to raise or lower your voice(s).

The Kraken

Below the thunders of the upper deep;
Far far beneath in the abysmal sea,
His ancient, dreamless, uninvaded sleep,
The Kraken sleepeth : faintest sunlights flee
About his shadowy sides: above him swell
Huge sponges of millennial growth and height;
And far away into the sickly light,
From many a wondrous grot and secret cell
Unnumber'd and enormous polypi
Winnow with giant fins the slumbering green.
There hath he lain for ages and will lie
Battening upon huge sea-worms in his sleep,
Until the latter fire shall heat the deep;
Then once by men and angels to be seen,
In roaring he shall rise and on the surface die.

Note: **The Kraken was a mythical Scandinavian sea-monster.**

"The Kraken" by Polina Bakhnova, a year thirteen student.

After the Performance

In small groups

- Pick out the words and phrases which you feel give this piece its distinctive mood and character. Concentrate upon the sounds and rhythm of the words rather than their meanings.
- Imagine making an animated version of this poem. What colours would you use? What kind of music would you use to accompany it? There is very little physical description of the Kraken. Why do you think this is? How would you present the creature in your animation?
- Examine the structure of the poem.
  How many syllables are there in each line?
  How many syllables in each line are stressed?
  How would you describe the rhyme-pattern of the poem?
- How do you think Tennyson's control of rhyme and rhythm help to give the piece its impact?

Assignment

Two hours

☐ Here are the names of some other fabulous beasts and mythological characters:

Chimaera   Bellona (Goddess of War)   Pegasus   Leviathan
Ganymede ("the most beautiful boy ever born")   the Golem
Gog and Magog   Hydra   the Minotaur   the Gorgon   Scylla
Cerberus   the Cyclops   Circe   the Sirens   the Harpies
Beelzebub   the Dragon

Write a poem of your own about one of them (or invent a name of your own). Imitate as closely as you can the *tone, diction* and *form* of Tennyson's poem.

Then write a careful commentary on what you've written, describing the ways you've tried to adopt Tennyson's poetic manner and saying how successful you think you've been.

Alexander Pope

EPISTLE

Working in pairs, examine this verse-letter, written in the early years of the eighteenth century. Some words have been deleted. They are listed, in random order, on page 55. Which words do you think best fit which spaces?

Epistle to Miss Blount on her leaving the Town after the Coronation (1714)

As some fond virgin, whom her mother's ****
Drags from the town to **** country air,
Just when she learns to **** a melting eye,
And hear a spark, yet think no danger nigh;
From the dear man unwilling she must sever,
Yet takes one kiss before she parts for ever:
Thus from the world fair Zephalinda flew,
Saw others happy, and with sighs ****;
Not that their pleasures caus'd her discontent,
She sigh'd not that they ****, but that she *****.

   She went to plain-work, and to purling brooks,
Old-fashion'd halls, dull aunts, and **** rooks,
She went from ****, park, assembly, play,
To morning walks, and **** three hours a day;
To pass her time 'twixt reading and bohea,
To muse, and spill her **** tea,
Or o'er cold **** trifle with the spoon,
Count the slow clock, and dine exact at ****;
Divert her eyes with pictures in the ****,
Hum half a tune, tell stories to the 'squire;
Up to her godly **** after sev'n,
There starve and pray, for that's the way to ****,
   Some 'squire, perhaps, you take delight to rack;
Whose game is whisk, whose treat a toast in sack,
Who visits with a ****, presents you birds,
Then gives a smacking buss and cries,—No words!

spark: dashing young man
nigh: near

plain-work: ordinary needle-work (not embroidery)
purling: murmuring while they flow

bohea: poor quality, cheap tea

buss: rude or playful kiss

Or with his hound comes **** from the stable,
Makes love with nods, and **** beneath the table;   **Makes love:** courts, woos
Whose laughs are ****, tho' his jests are coarse,
And loves you best of all things—but his ****.
   In some fair evening, on your elbow laid,
You dream of triumphs in the **** shade;
In pensive thought recall the fancy'd scene,
See **** rise on ev'ry green;
Before you pass th'imaginary sights
Of lords, and earls, and **** and garter'd knights;
While the spread fan **** your closing eyes;
Then give one flirt, and all the vision flies.   **flirt:** to flick a fan
Thus vanish sceptres, coronets, and ****,
And leave you in lone woods, or empty walls.
   So when your slave, at some dead, idle time,
(Not plagu'd with headachs, or the want of rhime)
Stands in the streets, abstracted from the crew,
And while he seems to study, thinks of you:
Just when his fancy points your sprightly eyes,
Or sees the blush of soft Parthenia rise,
Gay pats my **** and you vanish quite;   **Gay:** a fellow-poet of Pope's
****, chairs, and coxcombs rush upon my sight;   **coxcombs:** fools, fops
Vext to be still in ****, I knit my brow,
Look sow'r, and hum a tune – as you may now.

Note: **Zephalinda** and **Parthenia** were Pope's pet names for the Blount sisters, Teresa and Martha.

Missing words

knees	care	went	croaking	op'ra	roll
pray'rs	hollowing	stay'd	solitary	horse	rural
wholesom	hearty	withdrew	dukes		balls
shoulder	noon	Heav'n	coffee	gun	coronations
Streets	town	garret	fire	o'ershades	

Thinking/Talking Points

- Make two columns, one headed "Town", the other "Country". Under each one, list the things and the feelings the speaker in the poem associates with each place.
- What impression of country-life is being presented to the reader? And of town-life? Which of the two do you feel the writer prefers? Give your reasons.

- Describe carefully the *form* of Pope's poem, i.e. the patterns of rhyme and rhythm which hold it together. How would you describe the *diction* and *tone* of his letter?

Assignment

Individual work: two hours

☐ Write a short letter in the form of a poem, written in a similar style to Pope's, which Miss Blount sends him, describing her feelings about her new life in the country.

Write a detailed commentary on your piece. What features of Pope's poem did you try to imitate in your letter? How successfully do you feel you did it?

Charles Dickens

from DOMBEY & SON

Here's the opening of Dickens's novel *Dombey & Son*, published in 1846. Read it through a few times to yourself.

Dombey sat in the corner of the darkened room in the great arm-chair by the bedside, and Son lay tucked up warm in a little basket bedstead, carefully disposed on a low settee immediately in front of the fire and close to it, as if his constitution were analogous to that of a muffin, and it was essential to toast him brown while he was very new.

Dombey was about eight-and-forty years of age. Son about eight-and-forty minutes. Dombey was rather bald, rather red, and though a handsome well-made man, too stern and pompous in appearance to be prepossessing. Son was very bald, and very red, and, though (of course) an undeniably fine infant, somewhat crushed and spotty in his general effect, as yet. On the brow of Dombey, Time and his brother Care had set some marks, as on a tree that was to come down in good time—remorseless twins they are for striding through their human forests, notching as they go—while the countenance of Son was crossed and recrossed with a thousand little creases, which the same deceitful Time would take delight in smoothing out and wearing away with the flat part of his scythe, as a preparation of the surface for his deeper operations.

Dombey, exulting in the long-looked-for event, jingled and jingled the heavy gold watch-chain that depended from below his trim blue coat, whereof the buttons sparkled phosphorescently in the feeble rays of the distant fire. Son, with his little fists curled up and clenched, seemed, in his feeble way, to be squaring at existence for having come upon him so unexpectedly.

"The house will once again, Mrs Dombey," said Mr Dombey, "be not only in name but in fact Dombey and Son; Dom-bey and Son!"

The words had such a softening influence that he appended a term of endearment to Mrs Dombey's name (though not without some hesitation, as being a man but little used to that form of address) and said, "Mrs Dombey, my—my dear."

A transient flush of faint surprise overspread the sick lady's face as she raised her eyes towards him.

"He will be christened Paul, my—Mrs Dombey—of course."

She feebly echoed, "Of course," or rather expressed it by the motion of her lips, and closed her eyes again.

"His father's name, Mrs Dombey, and his grandfather's! I wish his grandfather were alive this day!" And again he said "Dom-bey and Son," in exactly the same tone as before.

Those three words conveyed the one idea of Mr Dombey's life. The earth was made for Dombey and Son to trade in, and the sun and moon were made to give them light. Rivers and seas were formed to float their ships; rainbows gave them promise of fair weather; winds blew for or against their enterprises; stars and planets circled in their orbits to preserve inviolate a system of which they were the centre. Common abbreviations took new meanings in his eyes, and had sole reference to them: A. D. had no concern with anno Domini, but stood for anno Dombei—and Son.

Thinking/Talking Points

In pairs

- Discuss your first impressions of Dombey and of his world.
- What sort of place do you imagine this scene taking place in? Which words and phrases suggest that?
- If you were making a picture of this scene, how would you represent Dombey? Think about his height, his posture, his clothes. Which of Dickens's details help you to visualise him?
- If you were turning this into a scene to be acted, how would you present Mrs Dombey? What textual evidence would support your presentation of her?
- Sum up Dombey's attitude to his business in your own words.
- Which of these words would you choose to describe the *narrator's* tone of voice in this passage:

light-hearted	neutral	sombre	angry	critical
scathing	gentle	ironic	detached	impartial
comic	sneering	compassionate		contemptuous

  Add words of your own to any you have chosen.
- How do you think Dickens expects the reader to feel about Dombey and his Son at the end of this passage?

Assignment

Two hours: choose one

☐ Write an essay of about one thousand words in which you examine
   (a) the impression of Dombey which Dickens creates in this extract
       and
   (b) the way in which he does it.

☐ Write a paragraph or two which might follow the extract you have
   studied. See if you can preserve the narrative tone of voice as well
   as the mood which has been established, whilst developing the
   situation Dickens presents.

Write a commentary on your continuation, describing the features of
Dickens's style and theme which you have tried to imitate. Discuss
how successful you feel you have been, quoting from both Dickens's
piece and your own.

from DADDY

Preliminary Assignment

Individual study: two hours

☐ What pictures and associations does the word "Daddy" have for you? Jot down some notes about each of the following:

> clothes   colours   smells   places   shops   games
> furniture   sounds   food   photographs   music   holidays
> memories   hopes and fears ...

In what way(s) do you find the word "Daddy" different from the words "Father" or "Dad"?

☐ Choose one of the following assignments:
1 Write a poem called "Daddy".
2 Using pictures and/or words cut from magazines, make a collage which presents what the word "Daddy" suggests to you.

☐ When you have produced your "Daddy" pieces, you may like to share them with the class and/or discuss some of the associations, overtones, reflections the word "Daddy" aroused for different people in the group.

Second Assignment: Listening and Response

Two hours

Someone who has prepared it thoroughly should now read Sylvia Plath's poem "Daddy" once to the class. We recommend everyone listens to it with his/her eyes closed. The text of the poem is on page 176.

☐ Taking no more than five minutes, jot down whatever you can recall from the poem: words; phrases; pictures and sounds... Get down as many details as possible. The order in which you write them down doesn't matter. If you can't recall the exact words, try to capture the images, flavour, tone or colour of what you remember in your own words.

☐ Working in small groups, imagine that every copy of the poem you have heard has been destroyed. How much of the poem can your group reassemble? A chairperson should scribe on a large sheet of paper what each person remembers. You will probably find that what one person recalls triggers off other recollections.

Working together, improve on/develop each detail and discuss whereabouts in the poem you think it came: at the beginning, in the middle, towards the end...

The rhymes and rhythms may help you to shape the materials you have.

☐ Working as a whole class see how much of the poem you can reconstruct.

Third Assignment: Collage

Individual work: one hour

☐ You will need piles of colour supplements or other magazines; scissors; gluesticks; sheets of A2 card.

From what everybody has been able to recall, each make a collage which you feel captures the tone, mood and some of the imagery of Plath's poem.

Display the collages you have produced. Discuss what each of you included/represented and why.

If you produced a collage for the preliminary assignment, discuss the ways in which it was similar to/different from the ones produced in response to Plath's poem.

Fourth Assignment: Performing

Small groups: thirty minutes

☐ Experiment with ways of performing some moments from the poem. Try miming some fragments or having one person read out the words whilst the rest act out what the words suggest to them.

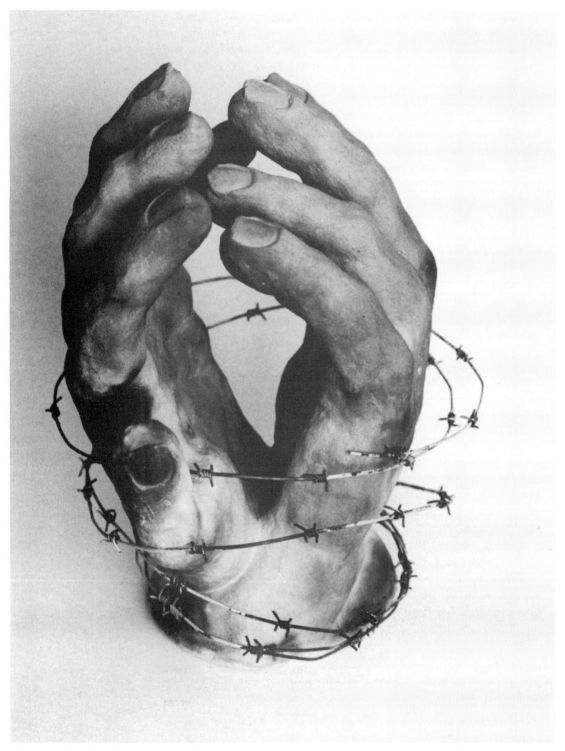

"Prisoner" by Tim Elcock, a year thirteen student.

Use sound effects you can make with your hands, feet and voices where you think that will make the moment more dramatic.

To begin with, you may like to experiment with different expression(s) and actions to suit these bits:

> Black shoe
> In which I have lived like a foot...
> Barely daring to breathe or Achoo
>
> The tongue stuck in my jaw
> It stuck in a barb wire snare
> Ich, ich, ich, ich.
>
> And I said "I do, I do"

Fifth Assignment: Writing

Individual work : two to three hours

Choose one

☐ "Daddy" has been described as "An exorcism in which there is a fine balance between hysteria and shrewd artistic control" (Fragine). How much of this do you agree with? Why?

Write an essay discussing this view of "Daddy" with close reference to a dozen or so details from the text.

☐ Describe the way Plath conveys the speaker's disturbed and contradictory feelings about her father in "Daddy". Look closely at particular images and the ways Plath exploits sounds, rhythms and changing tones of voice in her poem.

☐ Using Plath's poem as a model, compose a parallel/contrasting piece called "Mummy" or "Darling".

Write a commentary of about five hundred words explaining how your piece is similar to/different from Plath's. Refer closely to particular details in both pieces in your commentary.

☐ Turn to page 150 where you will find a student's response to the second question. Write a careful commentary on what the student has written, referring closely to the text of the poem. Where do you find yourself agreeing/disagreeing with what she has written?

Robert Browning

A DETECTIVE INQUIRY

Assignment

In pairs: one hour

☐ The facts of the case are problematic. There is a body. But when you are hunting for a murderer, you need to find a motive. And the clues are scattered: all the bits of the jigsaw are here but how do they fit together?

Here is the complete text of a work written about 1855. The fragments are mostly complete in themselves but they are tumbled across the pages in random order. See if you can reconstruct the piece as Browning wrote it. When it is in a recognisable and coherent form, see if you can unravel the mystery.

Try reading through the pieces as they are a few times, taking a fragment each in turn. Is there enough in each fragment to suggest the appropriate tone of voice? If there is, that may help you to see which pieces belong near one another.

And yet God has not said a word!

Porphyria worshipped me; surprise

> The smiling rosy little head,
> So glad it has its utmost will,
> That all it scorned at once is fled,
> And I, its love, am gained instead!

> The rain set early in tonight
> The sullen wind was soon awake,
> It tore the elm-tops down for
> And did its worst to vex the lake,

I propped her head up

she guessed not how
Her darling one wish would be heard.

Her hat and let the damp hair fall,

And I untightened next the tress
About her neck;

droops

burning

as before,

So, she was come through wind and rain
Be sure I looked up at her eyes
Proud,

Made my heart swell, and still it grew

her little throat around,

Porphyria's Lover

I listened with heart fit to break; When glided in Porphyria:

That moment she was mine

Three times

Porphyria's love:

again
Laughed the blue eyes without a stain.

Only, this time my shoulder bore
Her head, which   upon it still:

her cheek once more
Blushed bright beneath my   kiss:

spite,

and from her form
Withdrew the dripping cloak and shawl,
And laid her soiled gloves by,

untied

very proud; at last I knew

I found
A thing to do, and all her hair
In one long yellow string I wound

mine, fair,

While I debated what to do.

As a shut bud that holds a bee
I warily oped her lids:

Perfectly pure and good:

straight
She shut the cold out and the storm,
And kneeled

No   felt she;
I am quite sure she felt no

When no voice replied,
She put my arm about her waist,
And made her smooth white shoulder bare,
And all her yellow hair displaced,
And, stooping, made my cheek lie there,
And spread, o'er all, her yellow hair,
Murmuring

But passion sometimes would prevail, Nor could to-night's gay feast restrain A sudden thought of
one so pale For

pain

pain.

love of her, and all in vain;

And strangled her.

and made the cheerless grate, Blaze up

Which done, she rose,

And last, she sat down by my side
And called me.

how she loved me; she
Too weak for all her heart's endeavour,

To set its struggling   free
From pride, and vainer ties dissever,

passion

and all the cottage warm;

And give herself to me for ever:

And thus we sit together now,
And all night long we have not stirred,

William Shakespeare

from ANTONY AND CLEOPATRA

Shakespeare's play *Antony and Cleopatra* was written about 1606. Shakespeare drew most of the material for it from Sir Thomas North's translation of the first century Greek writer Plutarch's *Lives of the Noble Grecians and Romans.* North's English translation appeared in 1597.

The central characters in Shakespeare's play are the Roman general, Mark Antony, and the Egyptian queen, Cleopatra.

Here is Plutarch's account of Antony's first meeting with Cleopatra, in North's translation.

Read it through carefully a couple of times :

Therefore when she was sent unto by divers letters, both from Antonius himself and also from his friends, she made so light of it and mocked Antonius so much, that she disdained to set forward otherwise, but to take her barge in the river of Cydnus, the poop whereof was of gold, the sails of purple, and the oars of silver, which kept stroke in rowing after the sound of the music of flutes, howboys, citherns, viols, and such other instruments as they played upon in the barge.

And now for the person of herself: she was laid under a pavilion of cloth of gold of tissue, apparelled and attired like the goddess Venus, commonly drawn in picture: and hard by her, on either hand of her, pretty fair boys apparelled as painters do set forth god Cupid, with little fans in their hands, with the which they fanned wind upon her.

Her ladies and gentlewomen also, the fairest of them were apparelled like the nymphs Nereides (which are the mermaids of the waters) and like the Graces, came steering the helm, others tending the tackle and ropes of the barge, out of the which there came a wonderful passing sweet savour of perfumes, that perfumed the wharf's side, pestered with innumerable multitudes of people.

Here is Shakespeare's dramatisation of this passage.

The barge she sat in, like a burnish'd throne,
Burn'd on the water: the poop was beaten gold;
Purple the sails, and so perfumed that
The winds were love-sick with them; the oars were silver,
Which to the tune of flutes kept stroke, and made
The water which they beat to follow faster,
As amorous of their strokes. For her own person,
It beggar'd all description: she did lie
In her pavilion—cloth of gold, of tissue—
O'er-picturing that Venus where we see
The fancy outwork nature. On each side her,
Stood pretty dimpled boys, like smiling cupids,
With divers-colour'd fans, whose wind did seem
To glow the delicate cheeks which they did cool,
And what they undid did.

        O, rare for Antony!

Her gentlewomen, like the Nereides,
So many mermaids, tended her i' the eyes,
And made their bends adornings. At the helm
A seeming mermaid steers: the silken tackle
Swell with the touches of those flower-soft hands,
That yarely frame the office. From the barge
A strange invisible perfume hits the sense
Of the adjacent wharfs. The city cast
Her people out upon her; and Antony,
Enthron'd i' the market-place, did sit alone,
Whistling to the air; which, but for vacancy,
Had gone to gaze on Cleopatra too,
And made a gap in nature.

        Rare Egyptian!

Thinking/Talking Points

- Examine Shakespeare's lines carefully. What *exactly* has been added to North's version? What has been omitted? Discuss the effect of these additions and omissions.
- The most significant difference between the two extracts is that North's is in prose, Shakespeare's in blank verse. How does the *rhythm* of Shakespeare's writing modify and intensify the effect of

the information we are given? Pick out particular parts where you feel this is most noticeable.

Working the Text

- "Burn'd on the water" Try to picture this. Describe the various feelings the image conjures up.
- "Barge...burnished...burn'd...beaten..." What do you feel with these words coming so closely together?
- "Poop...purple...perfumed..." Do you think the effect of these alliterated words is similar to or different from the previous example?
- "Gold...purple...silver..." What do you associate with these colours? How does colour contribute to the impact of the passage as a whole?

- "The winds were love-sick..."
  "...the air... Had gone to gaze..."

What are we being made to feel about Cleopatra's power here and elsewhere in the passage?

- "the oars were silver,
  Which to the tune of flutes kept stroke"

Describe as fully as you can what you *hear* when you read these lines. What's the effect of Shakespeare's confining himself to flutes rather than the band North describes?

  (If you can, listen to the opening of Debussy's "L'Après-Midi d'un Faune".)
- Describe what happens to the water as the barge moves along. Notice how Shakespeare's control of *rhythm* and *tempo* here imitates the movement of the water.
- Why do you think Shakespeare gives us our first glimpse of Cleopatra so late in the passage?

- "her own person
  ...beggar'd all description"

What do you think this means? Why "beggar'd"?

- "cloth...gold...tissue"
          "the silken tackle
  Swell with the touches of those flower-soft hands"

Describe the various ways these details appeal to your senses. Which other details in the passage work in a similar way?
- Venus is the Goddess of Love. How do you imagine her? What pictures have you seen of her? How did you react to those?

What effects does Shakespeare generate in his lines which a painter could/could not match?

(Try to find in the library a print of Botticelli's picture of Venus and Mars. The original is in the National Gallery in London.)

- Describe in your own words the odd effects the "pretty dimpled boys" have on Cleopatra.
- How does the way Cleopatra's other attendants are described add to your impression of the scene?
- What is the effect of the glimpse of Antony we are given?

Read through North's and Shakespeare's versions again a few times before you choose your assignment.

Assignment

Choose one: two hours

☐ Write a careful study of how Shakespeare has adapted and dramatised North's words. Quote from both versions of the episode.

☐ Write a study of these lines, examining the variety of sensuous effects Shakespeare uses. What do you think is the dramatic impact of having these words spoken by a worldly-wise soldier?

☐ Produce a story-board of this speech or a collage which you feel captures the mood of Shakespeare's narrative.

Write a commentary on your artwork, describing what you were trying to do and the ways you went about it. Quote from Shakespeare's lines in your commentary.

☐ Examine these lines which come soon after the ones you have been studying. How do they add to/modify your impression of Queen Cleopatra?

> I saw her once
> Hop forty paces through the public street,
> And having lost her breath, she spoke, and panted,
> That she did make defect perfection,
> And, breathless, power breathe forth.

Oliver Goldsmith and Zoë Heller

A CITY NIGHT-PIECE *and* FEAR AND LOATHING AND PROZAC IN SOHO

Preliminary Assignment

Individual study: thirty minutes

☐ Write about a city you know well as you picture it at 2 a.m. Write in the first person; "I . . ." Begin the piece with you sitting in your room, imagining what may be going on about you in the city at that early hour. Then record what happens as you go out and walk the streets, noting what you observe and what you feel about what you see.

* * * * *

Goldsmith's "A City Night-Piece", is an example of the literary form called the essay: a self-contained piece of writing upon a theme of general human interest. Such pieces have featured in magazines from the eighteenth century to the present day. You'll find essays in most of today's Sunday newspapers and "serious" weekly and monthly magazines. It would be pretentious to describe such writing as "philosophical" or even "political". An essay may touch upon sensitive or contentious issues but its appeal is its limited, modest, educated-person-in-the-street common-sense approach delivered with a degree of elegance or charm.

Here's Goldsmith's essay which was first published in 1759.

The clock just struck two, the expiring taper rises and sinks in the socket, the watchman forgets the hour in slumber, the laborious and the happy are at rest, and nothing wakes but meditation, guilt, revelry, and despair. The drunkard once more fills the destroying bowl, the robber walks his midnight round, and the suicide lifts his guilty arm against his own sacred person.

Let me no longer waste the night over the page of antiquity, or the sallies of contemporary genius, but pursue the solitary walk, where Vanity ever changing, but a few hours past walked before me, where she kept up the pageant, and now, like a forward child, seems hushed with her own importunities.

What a gloom hangs all around! The dying lamp feebly emits a yellow gleam; no sound is heard but of the chiming clock, or the distant watch-dog. All the bustle of human pride is forgotten, an hour like this may well display the emptiness of human vanity.

There will come a time, when this temporary solitude may be made continual, and the city itself, like its inhabitants, fade away, and leave a desert in its room.

What cities, as great as this, have once triumphed in existence, had their victories as great, joy as just and unbounded, and, with short-sighted presumption, promised themselves immortality!—Posterity can hardly trace the situation of some. The sorrowful traveller wanders over the awful ruins of others; and, as he beholds, he learns wisdom, and feels the transience of every sublunary possession.

"Here," he cries, "stood their citadel, now grown over with weeds; there their senate-house, but now the haunt of every noxious reptile; temples and theatres stood here, now only an undistinguished heap of ruin. They are fallen, for luxury and avarice first made them feeble. The rewards of the state conferred on amusing, and not on useful members of society.

"Their riches and opulence invited the invaders, who, though at first repulsed, returned again, conquered by perseverance, and at last swept the defendants into undistinguished destruction."

How few appear in those streets which but some few hours ago were crowded! and those who appear, now no longer wear their daily masks, nor attempt to hide their lewdness or their misery.

But who are those who make the streets their couch, and find a short repose from wretchedness at the doors of the opulent? These are strangers, wanderers and orphans, whose circumstances are too humble to expect redress, and whose distresses are too great even for pity. Some are without the covering even of rags, and others emaciated with disease: the world has disclaimed them; society turns its back upon their distress, and has given them up to nakedness and hunger. These poor shivering females have once seen happier days, and are now turned out to meet the severity of winter. Perhaps, now lying at the doors of their betrayers, they sue to wretches whose hearts are insensible, or debauchees who may curse, but will not relieve them.

Why was I born a man, and yet see the sufferings of wretches I cannot relieve! Poor houseless creatures! the world will give you reproaches, but will not give you relief. The slightest misfortunes of the great, the most imaginary uneasiness of the rich, are aggravated with all the power of eloquence, and held up to engage our attention and sympathetic sorrow. The poor weep unheeded, persecuted by every subordinate species of tyranny; and every law which gives others security, becomes an enemy to them.

Why was this heart of mine formed with so much sensibility? or why was not my fortune adapted to its impulse? Tenderness, without a capacity of relieving, only makes the man who feels it more wretched than the object which sues for assistance.

Thinking/Talking Points

- What impact does the essay have on you? Do you think it is the one Goldsmith intended?
- What impression of the writer does the essay give you? Explain why.
- Jot down the details you can recall most vividly.
- The piece is written in the present tense. What do you think are the advantages/disadvantages of writing in this way?
- Which things has Goldsmith *observed* on this particular night? Which things does he *imagine* or *assume?*
- What do you understand by the word "vanity" as Goldsmith uses it here? What view of people does his use of that word imply?
- Look again at the passage which runs from "There will come a time"... to "undistinguished destruction". What effect do you feel Goldsmith is trying to achieve here? What means does he use to try to generate that effect? To what extent do you feel he is successful?
- What tone(s) of voice do you hear in the two concluding paragraphs?
- In what ways was Goldsmith's essay most/least like your own?

Second Assignment

Choose one: two hours

☐ Make an analysis of Goldsmith's essay, examining its structure and, referring to particular details, the various effects Goldsmith uses to engage the reader's interest and sympathies.

☐ Compare and contrast Goldsmith's essay with the following essay which appeared in *The Independent on Sunday* on 21 August 1994. Examine the similarities and differences between the *content* of the two essays and between *the impressions each gives us of the writer*. Quote fully from each essay in your study.

I have been depressed all week and consequently I have been holed up in my apartment like some kind of female Boo Radley. Every day I go get a coffee and a bagel from the deli and return to sit glumly at my kitchen table, failing to write anything until lunchtime. At around 12.30 or 1pm, I stagger into my bedroom for a protracted blubbing session on my bed. At 2pm—or, on bad days, 3pm—I decide to Pull Myself Together. I get up, sing karaoke to Jean Knight's "Mr Big Stuff"—Mr Big Stuff, who do you think you are? Mr Big Stuff! You're never gonna get my lerve, etc—and then, overcome with panic about deadlines, I lurch back to the kitchen table and begin the whole process once more.

On Thursday night I was due to attend a dinner party. I decided to go—partly because I did not seem to be responding well to solitary confinement, and partly because going to eat at another person's apartment is a rare thing in New York and I was genuinely excited at the prospect. While trying to get myself into some kind of presentable state for the occasion, I swallowed a couple of the Prozacs that a friend gave me a few weeks ago.

Now, of course, I knew in my sane mind that Prozac, however reportedly miraculous its results, could not be expected to transform me from a tear-stained W C Fields look-alike into a sunny-faced Pollyanna within a single evening. Had I applied reason, I would also have made the intelligent guess that Prozac is not compatible with alcohol. But whatever.—I took the Prozac, and of course my mood was not affected in any way: except that I developed a violent headache and found myself gripped by feelings of fear and loathing towards my fellow man.

The dinner party was truly grim. It was held in a SoHo loft full of art. There was a pair of shoes sitting in the middle of the floor, connected to the ceiling by a piece of wire. There was a collection of letters up on the wall, written by some old guy in the 1940s, when his wife was dying of pneumonia. They had been found in somebody's basement and the "artist" in question had had the genius idea of putting them in frames. This work was called *Excuse my Dust.* (The man whose loft it was spent a long time explaining the title, but I got so bored I went and sat in the lavatory until he had finished.) There were also some silver patterns on the wall that looked like the stuff you do with stencils when you're a kid. The loft owner informed me smugly that they were *actually* ancient Indian sexual signs repre-senting body parts in orgiastic situations. I had to stand there for ages, nodding my head, while he droned on about it: "So, like, this trape-zoid is an anus. ..." And all the while I was wondering what would happen if I were suddenly to lose control and shout, "I don't *care* about your putrid erotic murals, you dandified cretin—and if you say another word about them, I will chop your head off."

I knew I was being unreasonable because of feeling low—but still, the New York art world is pretty hard to take at the best of times.

About a month ago, I went to a party in another SoHo loft. This place was cluttered with racks of Mills and Boon paperbacks and giant plastic potted plants like you get in airports, and wall unit displays of porno magazines. It turned out that the hostess of this soirée, a red-haired woman in her early twenties, called Pagan or Axel or something, was an *artist* and all this horrible stuff was her *work*. Oh. Oh, how *interesting*.

She was bouncing around this party of hers urging her guests to play a game where you put on a blindfold and try to eat a marshmallow hanging by a piece of string from the ceiling. Boy, did I take a dislike to Pagan. She had an old factory time-clock up on the wall in her hallway, together with all the old punch cards of the people who used to work at the factory. This was another of her artworks—a witty tribute to the fascinating (and, let's face it, rather sexy) world of blue-collar labour. Pagan really did make you nostalgic for the days of compulsory national service.

Anyway, to get back to this week's dinner party. The host insisted on playing incredibly loud rock music. At one point, he asked me to put another record on. At the bottom of his pile of nasty rock CDs, I found a nice old Harry Belafonte tape. Everyone was outraged. It was "black music for white people" someone said, and all the other guests nodded sagely. I said I thought that (a) Harry Belafonte would be surprised to hear that and (b) if it was black music for white people, then it was altogether fitting, since everyone present was white. This line of argument did not go down well, and halfway through "Island in the Sun", the tape was rudely pulled out.

Then the host decided that he wanted to dance. Everyone in turn had to get up and cavort about the room with him to Prince's "The Most Beautiful Girl in the World" (which apparently counts as black music for black people). I decided it was time to leave.

The host felt that I owed him a long public goodbye snog. I did not. There was an unseemly tussle which everyone at the dinner table watched with a sort of silent, zombie fascination. After I had successfully fought him and his tongue off, my host turned nasty and said my new haircut made me look like an Avon lady. I smiled very sweetly and bade the company goodbye.

Back home, a family of mice had moved in while I was out, and one of them was scuttling about my bedroom. Along with everything else that Prozac wasn't doing for me, it certainly wasn't improving my attitude towards wildlife. I made a late night call to the building's superintendent, who wasn't picking up. I shouted menacing things at the mouse (which by this point I was beginning to think might be a rat). And then I gave up. As flies to wanton boys are we to the gods. I *had* planned to have a nice cosy cry before going to sleep, but I settled for standing on a chair and screaming instead.

Jane Austen

from SENSE AND SENSIBILITY

First Assignment: Dramatisation

In threes: ninety minutes

☐ Prepare a presentation of this chapter from Jane Austen's *Sense and Sensibility* as a radio broadcast. You may like to tape record your dramatisation.

Background Information

Mr John Dashwood promised his dying father "to do everything in his power" to make the lives of his three step-sisters and their mother comfortable. His infant son has just inherited Norland—a large estate—and as he is already very rich, Mr John Dashwood has decided to give each of his half-sisters one thousand pounds. He has convinced himself "he could spare so considerable a sum with little inconvenience". Jane Austen's ironic tone can be heard in the word "considerable". Considering how well-off Mr John Dashwood and his family have become, he is not being over-generous! In this chapter, Mrs John Dashwood encourages her husband to think again.

For the last ten years, Mr *John* Dashwood's three half-sisters and their mother, Mrs *Henry* Dashwood, have lived at Norland, looking after their aged uncle. They had expected, and deserved, to inherit the whole estate. But instead it has been left to Mr and Mrs *John* Dashwood's young son...

● Before you work on the extract which follows, discuss what you might expect Mrs John Dashwood to say to her husband about his decision.

Mrs John Dashwood now installed herself mistress of Norland; and her mother and sisters-in-law were degraded to the condition of visitors. As such, however, they were treated by her with quiet civility; and by her husband with as much kindness as he could feel towards anybody beyond himself, his wife, and their child. He really pressed them, with some earnestness, to consider Norland as their home; and, as no plan appeared so eligible to Mrs [Henry] Dashwood as remaining there till she could accommodate herself with a house in the neighbourhood, his invitation was accepted.

A continuance in a place where everything reminded her of former delight, was exactly what suited her mind. In seasons of cheerfulness, no temper could be more cheerful than hers, or possess, in a greater degree, that sanguine expectation of happiness which is happiness itself. But in sorrow she must be equally carried away by her fancy, and as far beyond consolation as in pleasure she was beyond alloy.

Mrs John Dashwood did not at all approve of what her husband intended to do for his sisters. To take three thousand pounds from the fortune of their dear little boy, would be impoverishing him to the most dreadful degree. She begged him to think again on the subject. How could he answer it to himself to rob his child and his only child too, of so large a sum? And what possible claim could the Miss Dashwoods, who were related to him only by half blood, which she considered as no relationship at all, have on his generosity to so large an amount. It was very well known that no affection was ever supposed to exist between the children of any man by different marriages; and why was he to ruin himself, and their poor little Harry, by giving away all his money to his half sisters?

"It was my father's last request to me," replied her husband, "that I should assist his widow and daughters."

"He did not know what he was talking of, I dare say; ten to one but he was light-headed at the time. Had he been in his right senses, he could not have thought of such a thing as begging you to give away half your fortune from your own child."

"He did not stipulate for any particular sum, my dear Fanny; he only requested me, in general terms, to assist them, and make their situation more comfortable than it was in his power to do. Perhaps it would have been as well if he had left it wholly to myself. He could hardly suppose I should neglect them. But as he required the promise, I could not do less than give it: at least I thought so at the time. The promise, therefore, was given, and must be performed. Something must be done for them whenever they leave Norland and settle in a new home."

"Well, then, let something be done for them; but that something need not be three thousand pounds. Consider," she added, "that when the money is once parted with, it never can return. Your sisters will marry, and it will be gone for ever. If, indeed, it could ever be restored to our poor little boy—"

"Why, to be sure," said her husband, very gravely, "that would make a great difference. The time may come when Harry will regret that so large a sum was parted with. If he should have a numerous family, for instance, it would be a very convenient addition."

"To be sure it would."

"Perhaps, then, it would be better for all parties if the sum were diminished one half.—Five hundred pounds would be a prodigious increase to their fortunes!"

"Oh! beyond any thing great! What brother on earth would do half so much for his sisters, even if really his sisters! And as it is—only half blood!—But you have such a generous spirit!"

"I would not wish to do any thing mean," he replied. "One had rather, on such occasions, do too much than too little. No one, at least, can think I have not done enough for them: even themselves, they can hardly expect more."

"There is no knowing what they may expect," said the lady, "but we are not to think of their expectations; the question is, what you can afford to do."

"Certainly—and I think I may afford to give them five hundred pounds a-piece. As it is, without any addition of mine, they will each have above three thousand pounds on their mother's death—a very comfortable fortune for any young woman."

"To be sure it is: and, indeed, it strikes me that they can want no addition at all. They will have ten thousand pounds divided amongst them. If they marry, they will be sure of doing well, and if they do not, they may all live very comfortably together on the interest of ten thousand pounds."

"That is very true, and, therefore, I do not know whether, upon the whole, it would not be more advisable to do something for their mother while she lives rather than for them—something of the annuity kind I mean.—My sisters would feel the good effects of it as well as herself. A hundred a year would make them all perfectly comfortable."

His wife hesitated a little, however, in giving her consent to this plan.

"To be sure," said she, "it is better than parting with fifteen hundred pounds at once. But then if Mrs Dashwood should live fifteen years we shall be completely taken in."

"Fifteen years! my dear Fanny; her life cannot be worth half that purchase!"

"Certainly not; but if you observe, people always live for ever when there is any annuity to be paid them; and she is very stout and healthy, and hardly forty. An annuity is a very serious business; it comes over and over every year, and there is no getting rid of it. You are not aware of what you are doing. I have known a great deal of the trouble of annuities; for my mother was clogged with the payment of three to old superannuated servants by my father's will, and it is

amazing how disagreeable she found it. Twice every year these annuities were to be paid; and then there was the trouble of getting it to
them; and then one of them was said to have died, and afterwards it
turned out to be no such thing. My mother was quite sick of it. Her
income was not her own, she said, with such perpetual claims on it;
and it was the more unkind in my father, because, otherwise, the
money would have been entirely at my mother's disposal, without
any restriction whatever. It has given me such an abhorrence of
annuities, that I am sure I would not pin myself down to the payment
of one for all the world."

"It is certainly an unpleasant thing," replied Mr Dashwood, "to
have those kind of yearly drains on one's income. One's fortune, as
your mother justly says, is not one's own. To be tied down to the
regular payment of such a sum, on every rent day, is by no means
desirable: it takes away one's independence."

"Undoubtedly; and after all you have no thanks for it. They think
themselves secure, you do no more than what is expected, and it
raises no gratitude at all. If I were you, whatever I did should be done
at my own discretion entirely. I would not bind myself to allow them
any thing yearly. It may be very inconvenient some years to spare a
hundred, or even fifty pounds from our own expenses."

"I believe you are right, my love; it will be better that there should
be no annuity in the case; whatever I may give them occasionally will
be of far greater assistance than a yearly allowance, because they
would only enlarge their style of living if they felt sure of a larger
income, and would not be sixpence the richer for it at the end of the
year. It will certainly be much the best way. A present of fifty pounds,
now and then, will prevent their ever being distressed for money, and
will, I think, be amply discharging my promise to my father."

"To be sure it will. Indeed, to say the truth, I am convinced within
myself that your father had no idea of your giving them any money at
all. The assistance he thought of, I dare say, was only such as might be
reasonably expected of you; for instance, such as looking out for a
comfortable small house for them, helping them to move their things,
and sending them presents of fish and game, and so forth, whenever
they are in season. I'll lay my life that he meant nothing farther;
indeed it would be very strange and unreasonable if he did. Do but
consider, my dear Mr Dashwood, how excessively comfortable your
mother-in-law and her daughters may live on the interest of seven
thousand pounds, besides the thousand pounds belonging to each of
the girls, which brings them in fifty pounds a-year a-piece, and, of
course,they will pay their mother for their board out of it. Altogether,
they will have five hundred a-year amongst them, and what on earth
can four women want for more than that?—They will live so cheap!
Their housekeeping will be nothing at all.

They will have no carriage, no horses, hardly any servants; they will keep no company, and can have no expenses of any kind! Only conceive how comfortable they will be! Five hundred a-year! I am sure I cannot imagine how they will spend half of it; and as to your giving them more, it is quite absurd to think of it. They will be much more able to give you something."

"Upon my word," said Mr Dashwood, "I believe you are perfectly right. My father certainly could mean nothing more by his request to me than what you say. I clearly understand it now, and I will strictly fulfil my engagement by such acts of assistance and kindness to them as you have described. When my mother removes into another house my services shall be readily given to accommodate her as far as I can. Some little present of furniture too may be acceptable then."

"Certainly," returned Mrs John Dashwood. "But, however, one thing must be considered. When your father and mother moved to Norland, though the furniture of Stanhill was sold, all the china, plate, and linen was saved, and is now left to your [step] mother. Her house will therefore be almost completely fitted up as soon as she takes it."

"That is a material consideration undoubtedly. A valuable legacy indeed! And yet some of the plate would have been a very pleasant addition to our own stock here."

"Yes; and the set of breakfast china is twice as handsome as what belongs to this house. A great deal too handsome, in my opinion, for any place they can ever afford to live in. But, however, so it is. Your father thought only of them. And I must say this: that you owe no particular gratitude to him, nor attention to his wishes, for we very well know that if he could, he would have left almost everything in the world to them."

The argument was irresistible. It gave to his intentions whatever of decision was wanting before; and he finally resolved, that it would be absolutely unnecessary, if not highly indecorous, to do more for the widow and children of his father, than such kind of neighbourly acts as his own wife pointed out.

Narrative Irony

This chapter from *Sense and Sensibility* illustrates a literary technique critics call *narrative irony*. It is a favourite device of, among others, Chaucer, Jane Austen, George Eliot, Henry James, Edith Wharton and T S Eliot. You will find further examples of this technique being used on pages 85, 97, 128, and 133.

Narrative irony is the trick of presenting what people say in such a way that we find their attitudes ridiculous or despicable even though the writer appears to be presenting their views in a completely detached and neutral way. The author does not criticise the characters' behaviour directly: that is left to the reader to do. Narrative irony uses understatement and innuendo to make its points. It is very different from the very direct way Dickens controls our attitudes to his characters, for example in the passage on page 32.

Second Assignment

Two hours

How do you think Mr and Mrs John Dashwood want to see themselves (and be seen by other people) at the end of this chapter? How do *you* see them? Look through the chapter carefully and pick out about a dozen words and phrases which you find force you to see Mr and Mrs John Dashwood's behaviour very differently from the way they'd like it to be seen.

If you have presented the piece as a piece of radio-drama, you will have noticed that it is not so much *what is said* which makes us dislike them. It is the *tone of voice in which it is said* which reveals them as hypocrites.

☐ Write a study of about one thousand words, examining the ways in which Jane Austen uses narrative irony to shape the reader's feelings about Mr and Mrs John Dashwood in this chapter. Quote freely from the chapter in your essay.

Charles Dickens

from HARD TIMES

Here are two further extracts from Dickens's novel *Hard Times*, published in 1854. You may wish to turn back to page 33 to remember how the novel begins.

Working in pairs, read through these passages silently a couple of times then read them aloud, taking a paragraph each in turn. Allow yourselves an hour to do this and to work through the Thinking/Talking Points.

It was a town of red brick, or of brick that would have been red if the smoke and ashes had allowed it; but, as matters stood it was a town of unnatural red and black like the painted face of a savage. It was a town of machinery and tall chimneys, out of which interminable serpents of smoke trailed themselves for ever and ever, and never got uncoiled. It had a black canal in it, and a river that ran purple with ill-smelling dye, and vast piles of building full of windows where there was a rattling and a trembling all day long, and where the piston of the steam-engine worked monotonously up and down, like the head of an elephant in a state of melancholy madness. It contained several large streets all very like one another, and many small streets still more like one another, inhabited by people equally like one another, who all went in and out at the same hours, with the same sound upon the same pavements, to do the same work, and to whom every day was the same as yesterday and tomorrow, and every year the counterpart of the last and the next...

A sunny midsummer day. There was such a thing sometimes, even in Coketown.

Seen from a distance in such weather, Coketown lay shrouded in a haze of its own, which appeared impervious to the sun's rays... The streets were hot and dusty on the summer day, and the sun was so bright that it even shone through the heavy vapour drooping over Coketown, and could not be looked at steadily. Stokers emerged from low underground doorways into factory yards, and sat on steps, and posts, and palings, wiping their swarthy visages, and contemplating coals. The whole town seemed to be frying in oil. There was a stifling smell of hot oil everywhere. The steam-engines shone with it, the dresses of the Hands were soiled with it, the mills throughout their many storeys oozed and trickled it. The atmosphere of those fairy palaces was like the breath of the simoom; and their inhabitants, wasting with heat, toiled languidly in the desert. But no temperature made the melancholy-mad elephants more mad or more sane. Their wearisome heads went up and down at the same rate, in hot weather and cold, wet weather and dry, fair weather and foul. The measured motion of their shadows on the walls, was the substitute Coketown had to show for the shadows of rustling woods; while, for the summer hum of insects, it could offer, all the year round, from the dawn of Monday to the night of Saturday, the whirr of shafts and wheels.

Drowsily they whirred all through this sunny day, making the passenger more sleepy and more hot as he passed the humming walls of the mills. Sunblinds, and sprinklings of water, a little cooled the main streets and the shops; but the mills, and the courts and alleys, baked at a fierce heat.

Down upon the river that was black and thick with dye, some Coketown boys who were at large—a rare sight there—rowed a crazy boat, which made a spumous track upon the water as it jogged along, while every dip of an oar stirred up vile smells. But the sun itself, however beneficent, generally, was less kind to Coketown than hard frost, and rarely looked intently into any of its closer regions without engendering more death than life.

Thinking/Talking Points

- Put the passages on one side. Jot down twenty descriptive details you can remember. Why do you think you remembered those details particularly? What feelings did those images give you?
- If you had not been told these passages came from the same novel as you looked at on page 33, would you have guessed? Why?
- Pick out all the phrases which describe the people who live in Coketown. Taken together, what impression are we given of the inhabitants? Who is giving us this impression? What do you think his/her motives are for presenting them in this way?

  If you were to turn this passage into an animated film, how would you represent the "Hands"? How would they move?
- Look again at the section in which Dickens describes a summer's day in Coketown. Why is such a day more terrible for its inhabitants than the coldest day in winter?
- How do you feel as you watch the boys rowing their "crazy boat"? See if you can describe how Dickens controls your feelings in the way he presents this episode.

- Pick just ten details from the passage which you think give the most powerful impression of the town. Write them out as "A Coketown Poem". Compare your poem with what other pairs have written.

Assignments

Choose one: two hours

☐ Imagine you are making a film of *Hard Times*. Choose one section from the extract above and make a story-board for it. Use brief quotations as captions for each of your frames.

☐ What impression of the town and its inhabitants does Dickens give you in these extracts? Write an essay quoting the details which help to give you those impressions and examine the way Dickens's *diction, imagery, rhythm* and *sentence-structure* convey them to you.

☐ On page 155 you will find some students' responses to the second assignment. Read through Dickens's passages again and then look at what each of the students has written. What do you agree/disagree with in each of their essays? How do you think each of them could have been improved?

George Eliot

from MIDDLEMARCH

Preliminary Assignment

Individual work: one hour

☐ You are a gentleman in a nineteenth century novel. You have met
the young lady who is all you hope for in a wife and have spoken to
her guardian who is happy that you should propose marriage to
her. You decide a letter is the way to ask for her hand.

The opening of the letter is below. Your assignment is to
compose the rest, bearing in mind the following points:

A The letter needs to be written in the style of a nineteenth century
novel. You may like to browse through some nineteenth century
fiction in the library. Register a little of the language and
manners of the time. Think about vocabulary, the way people
expressed themselves—and about nineteenth century attitudes to
love and marriage.

B Think what you are trying to convey to the imaginary lady about
yourself, your feelings about her and about the prospect of being
her husband.

My Dear Miss Brooke,
            I have your guardian's permission to address you on a
subject than which I have none more at heart.

In groups: thirty minutes

☐ Read your letters to each other and discuss what each of you has
written. What themes, attitudes, turns of phrase, expectations and
assumptions (if any) do your letters have in common?

How do you think the woman in question might respond to each
of your letters? Are some more persuasive than others? Do some
reveal more than their authors perhaps intended about their true
feelings about marriage?

What impression of yourselves did you (consciously or unconsciously) project?

Individual work: one hour

When you have talked about the intended and unintended messages *your* letters have sent, consider the letter which George Eliot's Mr Casaubon sent Miss Brooke. Read it through quickly and then more slowly *a few times.* Underline or highlight what you feel are its most interesting, baffling or revealing phrases.

My Dear Miss Brooke,

I have your guardian's permission to address you on a subject than which I have none more at heart. I am not, I trust, mistaken in the recognition of some deeper correspondence than that of date in the fact that a consciousness of need in my own life had arisen contemporaneously with the possibility of my becoming acquainted with you. For in the first hour of meeting you, I had an impression of your eminent and perhaps exclusive fitness to supply that need (connected, I may say, with such activity of the affections as even the preoccupations of a work too special to be abdicated could not uninterruptedly dissimulate); and each succeeding opportunity for observation has given the impression an added depth by convincing me more emphatically of that fitness which I had preconceived, and thus evoking more decisively those affections to which I have but now referred. Our conversations have, I think, made sufficiently clear to you the tenor of my life and purposes: a tenor unsuited, I am aware, to the commoner order of minds. But I have discerned in you an elevation of thought and a capability of devotedness, which I had hitherto not conceived to be compatible either with the early bloom of youth or with those graces of sex that may be said at once to win and to confer distinction when combined, as they notably are in you, with the mental qualities above indicated. It was, I confess, beyond my hope to meet with this rare combination of elements both solid and attractive, adapted to supply aid in graver labours and to cast a charm over vacant hours; and but for the event of my introduction to you (which, let me again say, I trust not to be superficially coincident with foreshadowing needs, but providentially related thereto as stages towards the completion of a life's plan), I should presumably have gone on to the last without any attempt to lighten my solitariness by a matrimonial union.

Such, my dear Miss Brooke, is the accurate statement of my feelings; and I rely on your kind indulgence in venturing now to ask you how far your own are of a nature to confirm my happy presentiment. To be accepted by you as your husband and the earthly guardian of your welfare, I should regard as the highest of providential gifts. In return I can at least offer you an affection hitherto unwasted , and the faithful consecration of a life which, however short in the sequel, has no backward pages whereon, if you choose to turn them, you will find records such as might justly cause you either bitterness or shame. I await the expression of your sentiments with an anxiety which it would be the part of wisdom (were it possible) to divert by a more arduous labour than usual. But in this order of experience I am still young, and in looking forward to an unfavourable possibility I cannot but feel that resignation to solitude will be more difficult after the temporary illumination of hope. In any case, I shall remain, yours with sincere devotion.

Edward Casaubon.

Thinking/Talking Points

In groups or as a class: one hour

- Discuss your initial impressions of the letter. Talk about its *diction, tone* and *shape.* How is this letter most/least like the one(s) you composed? What impression does it give you of Miss Brooke? And of Mr Casaubon?
- What do you notice about the frequency of personal pronouns (I, me, mine, ours, you) in this letter? What does that feature of his style suggest to you about the writer?
- Imagine you are Mr Casaubon. Describe to the rest of the group (a) your idea of marriage and your ideal wife and (b) what attracts you especially to Miss Brooke.
- Suggest what Mr Casaubon's profession might be. Explain why you think that. How does he feel about his work?
- Consider the *tone, diction* and *implications* of these words and phrases:

> your eminent and perhaps exclusive fitness to supply that need
> such activity of the affections
> thus evoking more decisively those affections to which I have but
>   now referred
> the commoner order of minds
> a capability of devotedness
> graver labours...vacant hours
> providentially related thereto as stages towards the completion of a
>   life's plan
> the accurate statement of my feelings
> an affection hitherto unwasted

- How do you expect Miss Brooke to feel as she reads the letter? What questions might she be asking herself?

Second Assignment

Individual work: one hour

☐ What impression of Edward Casaubon do you think George Eliot intends to convey to the reader of the novel? With close attention to particular details, examine the means by which she does it.

☐ Imagine yourself as Miss Brooke. Write a reply to Mr Casaubon's letter in what you think would be an appropriate style. Then write a commentary on what you have written, explaining how particular aspects of the style of the original letter have influenced the style of your own.

Third Assignment

Individual work or in pairs: two hours

☐ Paying close attention to particular words and phrases, write an essay examining these two passages from later in the novel:

My Dear Mr Casaubon,

      I am very grateful to you for loving me, and thinking me worthy to be your wife. I can look forward to no better happiness than that which would be one with yours. If I said more, it would only be the same thing written out at greater length, for I cannot now dwell on any other thought than that I may be through life, yours devotedly,

    Dorothea Brooke.

    Mr Casaubon, as might be expected, spent a great deal of his time at the Grange in these weeks, and the hindrance which courtship occasioned to the progress of his great work—The Key To All Mythologies—naturally made him look forward the more eagerly to the happy termination of courtship. But he had deliberately incurred the hindrance, having made up his mind that it was now time for him to adorn his life with the graces of female companionship, to irradiate the gloom which fatigue was apt to hang over the intervals of studious labour with the play of female fancy, and to secure in this, his culminating age, the solace of female tendance for his declining years? Hence he had determined to abandon himself to the stream of feeling, and perhaps was surprised to find what an exceedingly shallow rill it was. As in droughty regions baptism by immersion could only be performed symbolically, so Mr Casaubon found that sprinkling was the utmost approach to a plunge which his stream would afford him; and he concluded that the poets had much exaggerated the force of masculine passion. Nevertheless, he observed with pleasure that Miss Brooke showed an ardent submissive affection which promised to fulfil his most agreeable previsions of marriage. It had once or twice crossed his mind that possibly there was some deficiency in Dorothea to account for the moderation of his abandonment; but he was unable to discern the deficiency, or to figure to himself a woman who would have pleased him better; so that there was clearly no reason to fall back upon but the exaggerations of human tradition.

Were they what you expected? Why?
What expectations do they invite for the success of the marriage?
How do you feel about Miss Brooke and her suitor? Why?
What do you think the author's attitude is to (a) Miss Brooke and to (b) Mr Casaubon? Give your reasons.

Alternative Third Assignment

In pairs or groups: two hours

☐ On page 158 you will find two students' responses to the assignments on page 88. Read each one through and make a detailed report on what each student has written, referring closely to George Eliot's text as you do so.

What do you think is strong in each of the responses? In what ways do you think each of them could be improved?

James Joyce

from A PORTRAIT OF THE ARTIST AS A YOUNG MAN

This extract comes from James Joyce's novel which was published in 1916.

Work in pairs, so that one can read while the other closes his or her eyes and listens.

The preacher's voice sank. He paused, joined his palms for an instant, parted them. Then he resumed:

—Now let us try for a moment to realise, as far as we can, the nature of that abode of the damned which the justice of an offended God has called into existence for the eternal punishment of sinners. Hell is a strait and dark and foul-smelling prison, an abode of demons and lost souls, filled with fire and smoke. The straitness of this prison house is expressly designed by God to punish those who refused to be bound by His laws. In earthly prisons the poor captive has at least some liberty of movement, were it only within the four walls of his cell or in the gloomy yard of his prison. Not so in hell. There, by reason of the great number of the damned, the prisoners are heaped together in their awful prison, the walls of which are said to be four thousand miles thick: and the damned are so utterly bound and helpless that, as a blessed saint, saint Anselm, writes in his book on similitudes, they are not even able to remove from the eye a worm that gnaws it.

—They lie in exterior darkness. For, remember, the fire of hell gives forth no light. As, at the command of God, the fire of the Babylonian furnace lost its heat but not its light, so, at the command of God, the fire of hell, while retaining the intensity of its heat, burns eternally in darkness. It is a never ending storm of darkness, dark flames and dark smoke of burning brimstone, amid which the bodies are heaped one upon another without even a glimpse of air. Of all the plagues with which the land of the Pharaohs were smitten one plague alone, that of darkness, was called horrible. What name, then, shall we give to the darkness of hell which is to last not for three days alone but for all eternity?

—The horror of this strait and dark prison is increased by its awful stench. All the filth of the world, all the offal and scum of the world, we are told, shall run there as to a vast and reeking sewer when the terrible conflagration of the last day has purged the world. The brimstone, too, which burns there in such prodigious quantity fills all hell with its intolerable stench; and the bodies of the damned themselves exhale such a pestilential odour that, as saint Bonaventure says, one of them alone would suffice to infect the whole world. The very air of this world, that pure element, becomes foul and unbreathable when it has been long enclosed. Consider then what must be the foulness of the air of hell. Imagine some foul and putrid corpse that has lain rotting and decomposing in the grave, a jelly-like mass of liquid corruption. Imagine such a corpse a prey to flames, devoured by the fire of burning brimstone and giving off dense choking fumes of nauseous loathsome decomposition. And then imagine this sickening stench, multiplied a millionfold and a millionfold again from the millions upon millions of fetid carcasses massed together in the reeking darkness, a huge and rotting human fungus. Imagine all this, and you will have some idea of the horror of the stench of hell.

—But this stench is not, horrible though it is, the greatest physical torment to which the damned are subjected. The torment of fire is the greatest torment to which the tyrant has ever subjected his fellow creatures. Place your finger for a moment in the flame of a candle and you will feel the pain of fire. But our earthly fire was created by God for the benefit of man, to maintain in him the spark of life and to help him in the useful arts, whereas the fire of hell is of another quality and was created by God to torture and punish the unrepentant sinner. Our earthly fire also consumes more or less rapidly according as the object which it attacks is more or less combustible, so that human ingenuity has even succeeded in inventing chemical preparations to check or frustrate its action. But the sulphurous brimstone which burns in hell is a substance which is specially designed to burn for ever and for ever with unspeakable fury. Moreover, our earthly fire destroys at the same time as it burns, so that the more intense it is the shorter is its duration; but the fire of hell has this property, that it preserves that which it burns, and, though it rages with incredible intensity, it rages for ever.

—Our earthly fire again, no matter how fierce or widespread it may be, is always of a limited extent; but the lake of fire in hell is boundless, shoreless and bottomless. It is on record that the devil himself, when asked the question by a certain soldier, was obliged to confess that if a whole mountain were thrown into the burning ocean of hell it would be burned up in an instant like a piece of wax. And this terrible fire will not afflict the bodies of the damned only from without, but each lost soul will be a hell unto itself, the boundless fire raging in its very vitals. O, how terrible is the lot of those wretched beings! The

"A Vision of Hell" by Polina Bakhnova, a year thirteen student.

blood seethes and boils in the veins, the brains are boiling in the skull, the heart in the breast glowing and bursting, the bowels a red-hot mass of burning pulp, the tender eyes flaming like molten balls.

—And yet what I have said as to the strength and quality and boundlessness of this fire is as nothing when compared to its intensity, an intensity which it has as being the instrument chosen by divine design for the punishment of soul and body alike. It is a fire which proceeds directly from the ire of God, working not of its own activity but as an instrument of Divine vengeance. As the waters of baptism cleanse the soul with the body, so do the fires of punishment torture the spirit with the flesh. Every sense of the flesh is tortured and every faculty of the soul therewith: the eyes with impenetrable utter darkness, the nose with noisome odours, the ears with yells and howls and execrations, the taste with foul matter, leprous corruption, nameless suffocating filth, the touch with redhot goads and spikes, with cruel tongues of flame. And through the several torments of the senses the immortal soul is tortured eternally in its very essence amid the leagues upon leagues of glowing fires kindled in the abyss by the offended majesty of the Omnipotent God and fanned into everlasting and ever-increasing fury by the breath of the anger of the God-head.

—Consider finally that the torment of this infernal prison is increased by the company of the damned themselves. Evil company on earth is so noxious that the plants, as if by instinct, withdraw from the company of whatsoever is deadly or hurtful to them. In hell all laws are overturned—there is no thought of family or country, of ties, of relationships. The damned howl and scream at one another, their torture and rage intensified by the presence of beings tortured and raging like themselves. All sense of humanity is forgotten. The yells of the suffering sinners fill the remotest corners of the vast abyss. The mouths of the damned are full of blasphemies against God and of hatred for their fellow sufferers and of curses against those souls which were their accomplices in sin. In olden times it was the custom to punish the parricide, the man who had raised his murderous hand against his father, by casting him into the depths of the sea in a sack in which were placed a cock, a monkey, and a serpent. The intention of those law-givers who framed such a law, which seems cruel in our times, was to punish the criminal by the company of hurtful and hateful beasts. But what is the fury of those dumb beasts compared with the fury of execration which bursts from the parched lips and aching throats of the damned in hell when they behold in their companions in misery those who aided and abetted them in sin, those whose words sowed the first seeds of evil thinking and evil living in their minds, those whose immodest suggestions led them on to sin, those whose eyes tempted and allured them from the path of virtue. They turn upon those accomplices and upbraid them and curse them.

But they are helpless and hopeless: it is too late now for repentance.

—Last of all consider the frightful torment to those damned souls, tempters and tempted alike, of the company of the devils. These devils will afflict the damned in two ways, by their presence and by their reproaches. We can have no idea of how horrible these devils are. Saint Catherine of Siena once saw a devil and she has written that, rather than look again for one single instant on such a frightful monster, she would prefer to walk until the end of her life along a track of red coals. These devils, who were once beautiful angels, have become as hideous and ugly as they once were beautiful. They mock and jeer at the lost souls whom they dragged down to ruin. It is they, the foul demons, who are made in hell the voices of conscience. Why did you sin? Why did you lend an ear to the temptings of friends? Why did you turn aside from your pious practices and good works? Why did you not shun the occasions of sin? Why did you not leave that evil companion? Why did you not give up that lewd habit, that impure habit? Why did you not listen to the counsels of your confessor? Why did you not, even after you had fallen the first or the second or the third or the fourth or the hundredth time, repent of your evil ways and turn to God who only waited for your repentance to absolve you of your sins? Now the time for repentance has gone by. Time is, time was, but time shall be no more! Time was to sin in secrecy, to indulge in that sloth and pride, to covet the unlawful, to yield to the promptings of your lower nature, to live like the beasts of the field, nay worse than the beasts of the field, for they, at least, are but brutes and have no reason to guide them: time was, but time shall be no more. God spoke to you by so many voices, but you would not hear. You would not crush that pride and anger in your heart, you would not restore those ill-gotten goods, you would not obey the precepts of your holy church nor attend to your religious duties, you would not abandon those wicked companions, you would not avoid those dangerous temptations. Such is the language of those fiendish tormentors, words of taunting and of reproach, of hatred and of disgust. Of disgust, yes! For even they, the very devils, when they sinned, sinned by such a sin as alone was compatible with such angelical natures, a rebellion of the intellect: and they, even they, the foul devils must turn away, revolted and disgusted, from the contemplation of those unspeakable sins by which degraded man outrages and defiles the temple of the Holy Ghost, defiles and pollutes himself.

—O, my dear little brothers in Christ, may it never be our lot to hear that language! May it never be our lot, I say! In the last day of terrible reckoning I pray fervently to God that not a single soul of those who are in this chapel today may be found among those miserable beings whom the Great Judge shall command to depart for ever from His sight, that not one of us may ever hear ringing in his ears the awful sentence of rejection: *Depart from me, ye cursed, into everlasting fire which was prepared for the devil and his angels!*

He came down the aisle of the chapel, his legs shaking and the scalp of his head trembling as though it had been touched by ghostly fingers. He passed up the staircase and into the corridor along the walls of which the overcoats and waterproofs hung like gibbeted malefactors, headless and dripping and shapeless. And at every step he feared that he had already died, that his soul had been wrenched forth of the sheath of his body, that he was plunging headlong through space.

He could not grip the floor with his feet and sat heavily at his desk, opening one of his books at random and poring over it. Every word for him. It was true. God was almighty. God could call him now, call him as he sat at his desk, before he had time to be conscious of the summons. God had called him. Yes? What? Yes? His flesh shrank together as it felt the approach of the ravenous tongues of flames, dried up as it felt about it the swirl of stifling air. He had died. Yes. He was judged. A wave of fire swept through his body: the first. Again a wave. His brain began to glow. Another. His brain was simmering and bubbling within the cracking tenements of the skull. Flames burst forth from his skull like a corolla, shrieking like voices:—Hell! Hell! Hell! Hell! Hell!

Thinking/Talking Points

In pairs

- Put the text to one side. Jot down as many details as you can from memory. Do not worry about having them in the correct order. Aim to list twenty-five details between you.
- Turn back to the text. In the final paragraph Joyce describes a mixture of feelings running through the boy's head. How would you describe the boy's state of mind? Which phrases in this paragraph do you find the most evocative? What makes each one powerful? Is it the *rhythm*, the *diction*, the mixture of *images* or what?
- Do you think the boy is feeling the way the priest hoped his "little brothers in Christ" would be feeling after the address? What are your feelings about the priest, his intentions and his methods? Give your reasons.
- Now work through the whole passage, picking out twenty or so details which you feel work most powerfully upon the imagination.
- "Hyperbole" is the technical term for exaggeration. Too much hyperbole can be counter-productive. Instead of being horrified, we begin to laugh. You will have seen horror films which had this effect on you. How successful do you feel Joyce has been in sustaining the horror in this passage?

Assignments

Choose one: two hours

☐ Produce a picture (using any medium you like), drawing upon some of the images in this passage.

☐ In Shakespeare's *Hamlet* (Act 1 scene v) a ghost appears and says:

>   My hour is almost come,
> When I to sulphurous and tormenting flames
> Must render up myself.
>   ... But that I am forbid
> To tell the secrets of my prison house,
> I could a tale unfold whose lightest word
> Would harrow up thy soul, freeze thy young blood,
> Make thy two eyes, like stars, start from their spheres,
> Thy knotted and combined locks to part,
> And each particular hair to stand on end,
> Like quills upon the fretful porcupine.

Using some of the material from Joyce's passage, write a speech of up to two minutes' duration to replace the one Shakespeare gives his ghost. Use verse or prose, in either a contemporary or period style.

☐ Write a critical study of this extract from *Portrait of the Artist as a Young Man* examining what you think Joyce's purposes are in presenting the young boy's experience and commenting on his degree of success. Use plenty of brief quotations in your answer. Examine the impact of particular details upon you, the reader. How does the passage make you feel about the idea of hell, about the boy, about the priest and about the author?

Research assignment

Two to three hours

☐ Compare and contrast this sermon with the one given by Dinah Morris in Chapter Two of George Eliot's *Adam Bede*. Describe the contrasting impressions of their preachers George Eliot and James Joyce give you. Examine the details which you feel created those impressions.

T S Eliot

PORTRAIT OF A LADY

Consider what moderation is required to express oneself so briefly.

You can stretch every glance out into a poem, every sigh into a novel.

But to express a novel in a single gesture, a joy in a breath– such concentration can be present only in proportion to the absence of self-pity.

Schönberg on **Webern's** "Bagatellen" Opus 9 (1924)

Thinking/Talking Points

In pairs: thirty minutes

- What kind of poem does the title "Portrait of a Lady" lead you to expect?

   Would any of these titles lead you to expect the same *kind* of poem?

   Why?

The Lady Caught	Snapshot	A Woman Glimpsed
A Lady	The Lady and Me	A Lady Observed
Portrait D'une Femme	How I Saw Her	She

First Preliminary Assignment

Choose one: one hour

☐ Write a poem called "Portrait of a Lady" using what you think would be an appropriate kind of language and poetic form.

☐ Make a collage suggested to you by the title "Portrait of a Lady" using pictures cut from newspapers and magazines.

Second Preliminary Assignment

One hour

☐ Here are some words and phrases from the poem you will be working on. Make a copy of the chart below, writing out the quotations on the left-hand side. On the right-hand side, write down whatever associations the words have for you. We have shown you how one student filled in some of her chart but the quotations will probably have very different associations for you.

Quotation	Associations
a December afternoon Juliet's tomb Chopin	Romantic death of a lovely young couple. Piano lessons on Thursday evenings; boiled fish.
resurrected remote cornets cauchemar tom-tom capricious tobacco trance public clocks Paris in the Spring Achilles's heel journey's end the sporting page A Greek was murdered a street piano bric a brac expression in a glass a dancing bear pen in hand "dying fall"	Don't know what this means. Smoker's hut. Smelly but friendly. Gran's funeral. Hearses and hankies. Agamemnon?

Read through (or listen to) the following poem three or four times before considering the questions which follow. You may like to use two speakers: one for the narrator and another for the Lady.

Portrait of a Lady

I

Among the smoke and fog of a December afternoon
You have the scene arrange itself—as it will seem to do—
With "I have saved this afternoon for you";
And four wax candles in the darkened room,
Four rings of light upon the ceiling overhead,   5
An atmosphere of Juliet's tomb
Prepared for all the things to be said, or left unsaid.
We have been, let us say, to hear the latest Pole
Transmit the Preludes, through his hair and finger-tips.
"So intimate, this Chopin, that I think his soul   10
Should be resurrected only among friends
Some two or three, who will not touch the bloom
That is rubbed and questioned in the concert room."
—And so the conversation slips
Among velleities and carefully caught regrets   15   **velleities:** faint indications
Through attenuated tones of violins   **attentuated:** hushed
Mingled with remote cornets   **cornets:** small trumpets
And begins.
"You do not know how much they mean to me, my friends,
And how, how rare and strange it is, to find   20
In a life composed so much, so much of odds and ends,
(For indeed I do not love it ...you knew? you are not blind! how
    keen you are!)
To find a friend who has these qualities,
Who has, and gives
Those qualities upon which friendship lives.   25
How much it means that I say this to you—
Without these friendships—life, what cauchemar!"   **cauchemar:** nightmare
                                                                       (French)

Among the windings of the violins
And the ariettes   **ariettes:** tunes
Of cracked cornets   30
Inside my brain a dull tom-tom begins   **tom-tom:** primitive drum
Absurdly hammering a prelude of its own,
Capricious monotone   **capricious:** cheeky,
That is at least one definite "false note".   unpredictable
—Let us take the air, in a tobacco trance,   35
Admire the monuments,

Discuss the late events,
Correct our watches by the public clocks.
Then sit for half an hour and drink our bocks.

bocks: beers

II

Now that lilacs are in bloom   40
She has a bowl of lilacs in her room
And twists one in her fingers while she talks.
"Ah, my friend, you do not know, you do not know
What life is, you who hold it in your hands";
(Slowly twisting the lilac stalks)   45
"You let it flow from you, you let it flow,
And youth is cruel, and has no remorse
And smiles at situations which it cannot see."
I smile, of course,
And go on drinking tea,   50
"Yet with these April sunsets, that somehow recall
My buried life, and Paris in the Spring,
I feel immeasurably at peace, and find the world
To be wonderful and youthful, after all."

The voice returns like the insistent out-of-tune   55
Of a broken violin on an August afternoon:
"I am always sure that you understand
My feelings, always sure that you feel,
Sure that across the gulf you reach your hand.

prevailed: succeeded

You are invulnerable, you have no Achilles' heel.   60
You will go on, and when you have prevailed
You can say: at this point many a one has failed.
But what have I, but what have I, my friend,
To give you, what can you receive from me?
Only the friendship and the sympathy   65
Of one about to reach her journey's end.

I shall sit here, serving tea to friends ...."

I take my hat: how can I make a cowardly amends
For what she has said to me?
You will see me any morning in the park   70

comics: cartoons
(American)

Reading the comics and the sporting page.
Particularly I remark
An English countess goes upon the stage.
A Greek was murdered at a Polish dance,
Another bank defaulter has confessed.   75

I keep my countenance,
I remain self-possessed
Except when a street-piano, mechanical and tired
Reiterates some worn-out common song   **Reiterates:** plays again
With the smell of hyacinths across the garden   80
Recalling things that other people have desired.
Are these ideas right or wrong?

III

The October night comes down; returning as before
Except for a slight sensation of being ill at ease
I mount the stairs and turn the handle of the door   85
And feel as if I had mounted on my hands and knees.
"And so you are going abroad; and when do you return?
But that's a useless question.
You hardly know when you are coming back,
You will find so much to learn."   90
My smile falls heavily among the bric-a-brac.   **bric-a-brac:** bits and pieces

"Perhaps you can write to me."
My self-possession flares up for a second;
This is as I had reckoned.
'I have been wondering frequently of late   95
(But our beginnings never know our ends!)
Why we have not developed into friends.'
I feel like one who smiles, and turning shall remark
Suddenly, his expression in a glass.   **glass:** mirror
My self-possession gutters; we are really in the dark. 100   **gutters:** goes out, like a
                                                               candle flame

"For everybody said so, all our friends,
They all were sure our feelings would relate
So closely! I myself can hardly understand.
We must leave it now to fate.
You will write, at any rate.   105
Perhaps it is not too late.
I shall sit here, serving tea to friends."
And I must borrow every changing shape
To find expression ... dance, dance
Like a dancing bear,   110
Cry like a parrot, chatter like an ape.
Let us take the air, in a tobacco trance—

Well! and what if she should die some afternoon,
Afternoon grey and smoky, evening yellow and rose;
Should die and leave me sitting pen in hand   115

> With the smoke coming down above the housetops;
> Doubtful, for a while
> Not knowing what to feel or if I understand
> Or whether wise or foolish, tardy or too soon ...
> Would she not have the advantage, after all?   120
> This music is successful with a "dying fall"
> Now that we talk of dying—
> And should I have the right to smile?

Notes:

"You are invulnerable, you have no Achilles heel": you have no weaknesses, no weak points.

Chopin wrote piano music in the early nineteenth century. His "Preludes" are among his most popular pieces. Each one is very brief and creates a particular mood or atmosphere, using very few notes. Try to listen to some of them if you can. T S Eliot used the same title "Preludes" for a poem he wrote about the same time as "Portrait of a Lady". That poem uses very few words to create a vivid sense of a day in the life of a modern city.

Thinking/Talking Points

In pairs or as a class

- Discuss your initial impressions of
  (a) the Lady
  (b) the narrator
  (c) the kind of world they live in
  (d) their "friendship"
  Pick out some of the words and phrases which helped you form those impressions.
- What period of time does the "plot" cover? How does the structure of the poem reflect this? See if you can summarise the story the poem tells in a hundred words.
- The poem tells us about a relationship between two people: the narrator and the Lady. Neither of them is given a name. What is different about the way Eliot presents each of his two characters?
- Pick out some moments in this poem where Eliot creates a strong sense of atmosphere using very few words. Describe what each of the descriptive details helps you imagine.
- What attitude does the *Lady* seem to have to Chopin and to the "concert-room" she and the narrator have been to? What does the *narrator's* attitude to the concert seem to be? Which phrases suggest

that? Do you think we are expected to agree with the way either of them feels about Chopin's music? Give your reasons.

- How many other references to various types of music can you find in the poem? Eliot uses them almost as a director might use music to accompany a film. Describe the way the musical references suggest different moods at different moments in the poem.

- Among the words used most often in the poem are "friend", "friends" and "friendship". What would your own definition of a "friend" be? Does the Lady treat the narrator as you would treat a friend? Give your reasons.

- Eliot never describes the Lady but he gives us a very strong impression of her from the way she speaks. Pick out a dozen things she says. Discuss what impression each one gives you of her outlook on life, her feelings about herself, about the narrator and about the kind of society she lives in. How do you think you would feel if this Lady were saying these things to you?

- The narrator never speaks, except to us. Why do you think Eliot decided to let us hear nothing of what he said to the Lady? What kind of person do you think the narrator sees him/herself as? At one point s/he uses this image :

> My self-possession flares up for a second...
> My self-possession gutters...

What does this image suggest to you about her or his self-confidence? Why exactly is the narrator "ill at ease" when s/he visits the Lady for the third time?

- How would you describe the different kinds of smiles we see in lines 49, 92 and 99?

- *Where* do you think the final eleven lines of the poem might be set? The narrator is trying to work out how she or he might feel if news arrived that the Lady had died. See if you can describe his or her mixed feelings about her in your own words?

- Do you think the narrator is male or female? Why? Is it possible to tell from the narrative?

- Eliot's poem begins not as we have printed it on page 99 but like this:

Portrait of a Lady

Thou hast committed – – –
Fornication: but that was in another country,
And besides, the wench is dead.

The Jew of Malta

This fragment comes from a play written by Marlowe in the sixteenth century. How would you describe Barabas's tone of voice and his attitude to the woman he is speaking about here:

SERVANT: Thou hast committed – – –
BARABAS: Fornication: but that was in another country,
                    And besides, the wench is dead.

What do you think is the relationship between the last line of Eliot's poem and this fragment from Marlowe's play?

• *Portrait of a Lady* is the title of a novel written in 1881 by an American novelist, Henry James, who lived in London. It is about six hundred pages long. Eliot was an American poet, living in London when he wrote this poem in 1917. Eliot knew James's work well. How many lines long is his poem? What do you think he might have been attempting to do in his poem? What were the advantages/disadvantages of using Henry James's well-known title?

Assignment

Choose one: two or three hours

☐ "Portrait of a Lady" has been described as a "compressed novel", Eliot using the fewest words possible to give us a very full insight into a relationship. Discuss *how* Eliot manages to use so little to suggest so much: about the Lady, about the narrator, about the world in which they live and about their "friendship".

   You may wish to examine the way he uses *rhythm, rhyme, diction* and particular *tones of voice* to achieve his effects.

☐ Describe the different ways Eliot presents the Lady (through her conversation) and the narrator (through her/his memories and reflections). What do you find effective or frustrating about Eliot's economical use of language?

☐ Imagine the Lady keeping a diary covering the period of her "friendship" with the narrator. Write a few entries in which she records her changing attitude to her/him. Try to convey that she is being less honest about her true feelings than she is aware of.

☐ Imagine yourself as the narrator. A telegram has arrived telling you that the Lady has died. Write something in which you to try record your lasting impressions of her: this might be in the form of a diary-entry, a letter to a friend, a letter to the Lady's daughter, an obituary for a newspaper or another poem.

☐ Compare and contrast Eliot's poem with Browning's "Last Ride Together" in any ways you find interesting.

William Shakespeare

from MEASURE FOR MEASURE

In pairs

Read this soliloquy from *Measure for Measure* to each other a few times
before considering the questions below.

Act II, scene ii, lines 162-187

ANGELO What's this? What's this? Is this her fault or mine?
The tempter or the tempted, who sins most?
Ha!
Not she; nor doth she tempt: but it is I
That, lying by the violet in the sun,
Do as the carrion does, not as the flower,
Corrupt with virtuous season. Can it be
That modesty may more betray our sense
Than woman's lightness? Having waste ground enough,
Shall we desire to raze the sanctuary,
And pitch our evils there? O, fie, fie, fie!
What dost thou, or what art thou, Angelo?
Dost thou desire her foully for those things
That make her good? O,let her brother live:
Thieves for their robbery have authority,
When judges steal themselves. What, do I love her,
That I desire to hear her speak again,
And feast upon her eyes? What is't I dream on?
O cunning enemy, that, to catch a saint,
With saints dost bait thy hook! Most dangerous
Is that temptation that doth goad us on
To sin in loving virtue: never could the strumpet,
With all her double vigour, art and nature,
Once stir my temper; but this virtuous maid
Subdues me quite. Ever till now,
When men were fond, I smiled, and wonder'd how.

virtuous: good, honest
modesty: restraint, not being a flirt
lightness: being a flirt, trying to seduce

goad: incite, push, force

stir my temper: excite, disturb, unsettle me, make me lose control

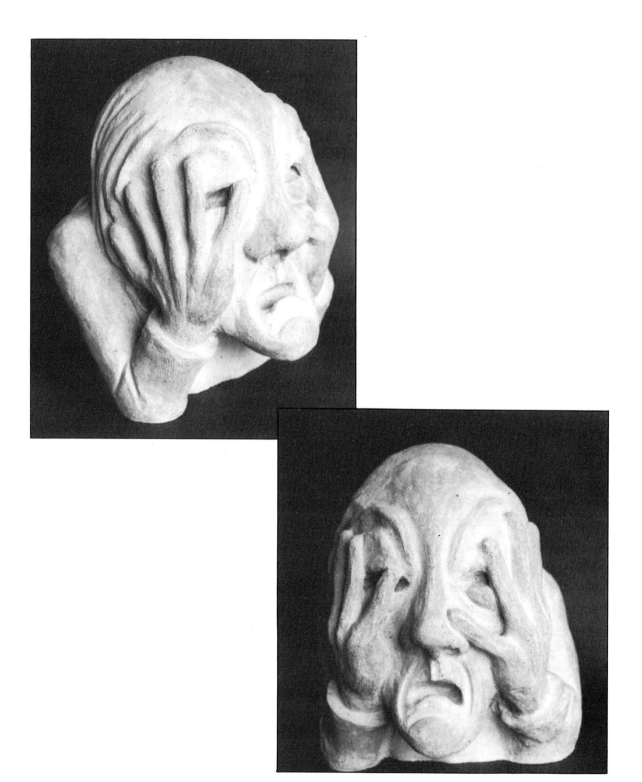

"Temptation" by Tim Elcock, a year thirteen student.

Working the Text

In pairs

- What can you deduce from this soliloquy alone about the speaker and the situation he finds himself in?
- What does the speaker's name suggest to you? What can you discover *from the soliloquy* about Angelo's social standing and his past life?
- What impression does the opening line give you of Angelo's state of mind? Where else in the passage does the punctuation give you a clue to Angelo's mood?
- What is the difference between a "tempter" and the one who's "tempted"? Angelo asks which of them "sins most". How would you answer that question? Describe a situation in which you might find yourself asking the question Angelo asks here.
- Angelo pictures carrion (dead flesh) "lying by" a violet in the sunshine. How does that image make you feel? What meaning(s) of "lying" do you think Shakespeare is using here?
- If carrion is "corrupt", it goes rotten, it stinks. Suggest more than one meaning for the word "season" here:

  > ...it is I
  > That, lying by the violet in the sun,
  > Do as the carrion does, not as the flower,
  > Corrupt with virtuous season.

- Which of the different meanings of the word "sense" are being used here?

  > Can it be
  > That modesty may more betray our sense
  > Than woman's lightness?

- A "sanctuary" is a safe, holy place. "Raze" means to demolish. The word "pitch" can have different meanings. What picture(s) do you imagine as you hear these words:

  > to raze the sanctuary,
  > And pitch our evils there?

- A paradox is a statement which seems to contradict itself. Angelo used one when he described the carrion as being corrupted by sunshine, which we usually think of as having a good effect. Explain the paradox here:

  > Most dangerous
  > Is that temptation that doth goad us on
  > To sin in loving virtue:

- In this soliloquy, Angelo is thinking about a woman. Which details give you the strongest impression of her personality?
- A "strumpet" is a prostitute. "Vigour" means "power" or "energy". What do you think Angelo means when he talks of a strumpet's having *double* vigour" from "art and nature"?
- What can you deduce from this passage about the situation the woman's brother is in? What does that add to your impression of Angelo?
- "Bait" is a tasty morsel a fisherman uses to catch a fish. Whom do you think Angelo is referring to when he speaks of the "cunning enemy"? What is cunning about him?
- The word "fond" here means "infatuated". What does the last sentence of his soliloquy add to your impression of the sort of person Angelo has been in the past? What kind of "smile" do you imagine?
- What do you think Angelo has learnt about himself and about the world in the course of this soliloquy?

Assignment

Two hours

☐ Read through Angelo's soliloquy again a few more times, picking out what you think are the most important and interesting details.

Then write an essay in which you examine the progress of Angelo's examination of himself and the situation he finds himself in here. In your essay, quote and comment as fully as you can upon at least half a dozen textual details.

Further Work

Two hours

Here are some other Shakespearean soliloquies you may enjoy working on. Choose one and explore the way Shakespeare presents the thoughts and state of mind of the speaker at that point in the play. See how much you can discover about the speaker and her/his situation without knowing more than the speeches themselves tell us.

Hamlet: I-ii, ll 129-159
Hamlet: III-iii, ll 36-72
Macbeth: I-vii, ll 1-28
Romeo & Juliet: IV-iii, ll 14-58
The Winter's Tale: I-ii, ll 108-146
The Tempest: V-i, ll 33-57
Timon of Athens: IV-i, ll 1-41

Toni Morrison

from THE BLUEST EYE

In small groups: one hour

Here is the opening of Toni Morrison's novel, *The Bluest Eye*, which
was first published in America in 1970.

   Read it through a few times together before considering the points
which follow. We suggest one person reads each paragraph.

Here is the house. It is green and white. It has a red door. It is very
pretty. Here is the family. Mother, Father, Dick, and Jane live in the
green-and-white house. They are very happy. See Jane. She has a red
dress. She wants to play. Who will play with Jane? See the cat. It goes
meow-meow. Come and play. Come play with Jane. The kitten will
not play. See Mother. Mother is very nice. Mother, will you play with
Jane? Mother laughs. Laugh, Mother, laugh. See Father. He is big and
strong. Father, will you play with Jane? Father is smiling. Smile, Father, smile. See the dog. Bowwow goes the dog. Do you want to play?
Do you want to play with Jane? See the dog run. Run, dog, run. Look,
look. Here comes a friend. The friend will play with Jane. They will
play a good game. Play, Jane, play.

Here is the house it is green and white it has a red door it is very
pretty here is the family mother father dick and jane live in the green-
and-white house they are very happy see jane she has a red dress she
wants to play who will play with jane see the cat it goes meow-meow
come and play come play with jane the kitten will not play see mother
mother is very nice mother will you play with jane mother laughs
laugh mother laugh see father he is big and strong father will you play
with jane father is smiling smile father smile see the dog bowwow
goes the dog do you want to play do you want to play with jane see the
dog run run dog run look look here comes a friend the friend will play
with jane they will play a good game play jane play

Hereisthehouseitisgreenandwhiteithasareddooritisveryprettyhereisthefa
milymotherfatherdickandjaneliveinthegreenandwhitehousetheyareyery
happyseejaneshehasareddressshewantstoplaywhowillplaywithjaneseethe
catitgoesmeowmeowcomeandplaycomeplaywithjanethekittenwillnotpla
yseemothermotherisyerynicemotherwillyouplaywithjanemotherlaughsla
ughmotherlaughseefatherheisbigandstrongfatherwillyouplaywithjanefat
herissmilingsmilefathersmileseethedogbowwowgoesthedogdoyouwantto
playdoyouwanttoplaywithjaneseethedogrunrundogrunlooklookherecom
esafriendthefriendwillplaywithjanetheywillplayagoodgameplayjaneplay

Quiet as it's kept, there were no marigolds in the fall of 1941. We thought, at the time, that it was because Pecola was having her father's baby that the marigolds did not grow. A little examination and much less melancholy would have proved to us that our seeds were not the only ones that did not sprout; nobody's did. Not even the gardens fronting the lake showed marigolds that year. But so deeply concerned were we with the health and safe delivery of Pecola's baby we could think of nothing but our own magic: if we planted the seeds, and said the right words over them, they would blossom, and everything would be all right.

It was a long time before my sister and I admitted to ourselves that no green was going to spring from our seeds. Once we knew, our guilt was relieved only by fights and mutual accusations about who was to blame. For years I thought my sister was right: it was my fault. I had planted them too far down in the earth. It never occurred to either of us that the earth itself might have been unyielding. We had dropped our seeds in our own little plot of black dirt just as Pecola's father had dropped his seeds in his own plot of black dirt. Our innocence and faith were no more productive than his lust or despair. What is clear now is that of all of that hope, fear, lust, love, and grief, nothing remains but Pecola and the unyielding earth. Cholly Breedlove is dead; our innocence too. The seeds shrivelled and died; her baby too.

There is really nothing more to say—except why. But since why *is difficult to handle, one must take refuge in* how.

Thinking/Talking Points

- Discuss your first impressions of this extract.
- How would you describe the style of the *opening* paragraph? What kind of writing does it seem to belong to?

  What tone of voice do you read it in? Think of some of the ways other people might read it.
- Now discuss the impact of the *second* and *third* paragraphs. How would you describe what is happening to the story? How do you feel as you read the three versions?
- Reread the rest of the first chapter. Talk about the possible meanings and impact of the phrase "Quiet as it's kept." Describe as

"Toyshop" by Vikki Hartley, a year thirteen student.

fully as you can to each other the situation the speaker tells us about. Which details do you think are most shocking/important/revealing?

- What impression of the speaker do those paragraphs give you? Which details shape that impression?
- Would you use any of these words to describe the *tone* of those paragraphs?

light-hearted	grim	savage	amused	sad	angry
forlorn	child-like	ironic	playful		wistful
confused	frustrated	bitter	dream-like		nervous
excited	disturbed	secretive	passionate...		

Add some of your own words.

Which words, phrases and ideas in these paragraphs do most to set the tone you hear in them?

- Now read the three opening paragraphs again. What *connections* do you think there are between them and what comes next?
- What do you notice about the use of colours in the first paragraph? In the light of what you have read and discussed, talk about the possible significance of the novel's title, *The Bluest Eye*.

- Discuss the impact the whole extract made on you. Can you suggest why Toni's Morrison began her novel as she did? How effective do you think it is?
- You may not know that Toni Morrison is a black American writer; she is a university professor; and in 1993, she won the Nobel Prize for Literature. Discuss whether/why these facts affect your "reading" of the passage.

Assignments

Choose one: two hours

☐ Prepare a performance of the opening of Toni Morrison's *The Bluest Eye* if possible to a group which has not seen the text. Experiment until you find what seems to you an effective way of presenting it. For example, you might wish to use acting, miming,dancing, singing, choral reading, audio or video recording.

☐ Make a collage called *The Bluest Eye*, using images cut from magazines and perhaps words suggested to you by this opening.

☐ Write an essay examining the impact on you of the opening of Toni Morrison's novel, *The Bluest Eye*. Describe what you feel the writer was trying to achieve by structuring the beginning of her novel in the way she did and the kind of novel this opening leads you to expect.

Quote extensively from the extract in your essay, discussing the impact of the writer's choice of *form, diction, rhythm, imagery* and *tone*.

☐ On page 163, you will find a student's response to the third assignment. Read it through and discuss the way the student has written about the piece. Write a report on the essay, saying what you most/least like about it and suggesting ways it might be developed.

Refer closely to Toni Morrison's opening chapter in your commentary.

William Shakespeare and Gerard Manley Hopkins

KING LEAR *and*
NO WORST, THERE IS NONE

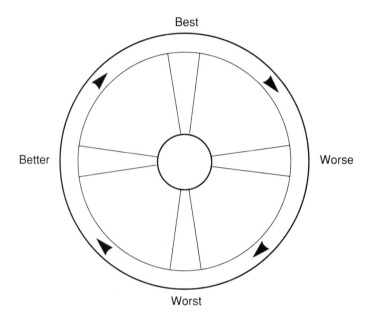

In this unit you will be exploring a poem written in the nineteenth century by Gerard Manley Hopkins. But because Hopkins's poem was probably influenced by it, the unit begins with a study of an episode from Shakespeare's *King Lear* written in the early seventeenth century.

Preliminary Study

One hour

What is the worst thing you can imagine happening to you?

Think carefully. Can you imagine nothing worse than that?

One of the themes of Shakespeare's *King Lear* is the terrible capacity of people for suffering. In the play, all the characters we respect are tormented beyond what most of us could endure.

Read the extracts that follow and then discuss the experiences Edgar and Gloucester undergo in this episode and the ways they respond to them.

Edgar, the son of Gloucester, takes stock of his situation. He has been falsely accused by his evil brother Edmund (whom he trusted) of plotting the death of their father. Edgar has had to flee for his life. Hunted high and low, he has escaped by disguising himself as Mad Tom, an almost naked and apparently mad beggar.

In Act III of the play, he had sheltered in a hovel during a violent storm and watched King Lear, driven mad by his daughters' cruelty, suffer both physically at the hands of the storm and mentally as he recalled his daughters' treatment of him. Now speaking in his normal voice, (Act IV, scene i) Edgar tries to cheer himself up by reflecting that he appears to have experienced as much misery as anyone can; things can only get better. If you are at the bottom of the Wheel of Fortune, you can only rise.

contemned: condemned	EDGAR

EDGAR

> Yet better thus, and known to be contemned,
> Than, still contemned and flattered, to be worst.
> The lowest and most dejected thing of Fortune
> Stands still in esperance, lives not in fear:
> The lamentable change is from the best;
> The worst returns to laughter. Welcome, then,
> Thou unsubstantial air that I embrace:
> The wretch that thou hast blown unto the worst
> Owes nothing to thy blasts.

dejected: downcast, sad
Fortune: the Goddess of Chance, Luck
esperance: hope
lamentable: sad
returns to laughter: is happy again.

At this point, as if to show Edgar and the audience how much more suffering a person can take, Shakespeare brings onto the stage a hideous figure. It is Edgar's father whose eyes have been torn out as a result of another of Edmund's ruthless schemes. The blinded Gloucester, led by a faithful old servant, is as tormented by realising how he has misjudged his two sons as by his physical pain.

EDGAR

> But who comes here?
> My father, poorly led? World, world, O world!
> But that thy strange mutations make us hate thee,
> Life would not yield to age.

poorly led: led like a wretched beggar
mutations: changes

OLD MAN

> O my good Lord!
> I have been your tenant, and your father's tenant,
> These fourscore years.

fourscore: eighty

GLOUCESTER

> Away, get thee away; good friend, be gone:
> Thy comforts can do me no good at all;
> Thee they may hurt.

OLD MAN   You cannot see your way.

GLOUCESTER   I have no way, and therefore want no eyes;
             I stumbled when I saw. Full oft 'tis seen,
             Our means secure us, and our mere defects
             Prove our commodities. Oh! dear son Edgar,
             The food of thy abused father's wrath;
             Might I but live to see thee in my touch,
             I'd say I had eyes again.

Full oft: very often

abused: tricked
wrath: anger

OLD MAN   How now! Who's there?

EDGAR *(aside)* O Gods! Who is't can say "I am at the worst"?
             I am worse than e'er I was.

OLD MAN   'Tis poor mad Tom.

EDGAR *(aside)* And worse I may be yet; the worst is not
             So long as we can say 'This is the worst.'

Note: **"Our means...commodities"**: we are careless when we're comfortable whereas bad luck often does us good.

Hopkins's sonnet, "No Worst, There Is None" seems to take not only its theme but some of its imagery from Edgar's reflections. Listen to someone who has prepared it read it aloud two or three times before looking at the points which follow:

No worst, there is none. Pitched past pitch of grief,
More pangs will, schooled at forepangs, wilder wring.
Comforter, where, where is your comforting?
Mary, mother of us, where is your relief?
My cries heave, herds-long; huddle in a main, a chief-   5
Woe, world-sorrow; on an age-old anvil wince and sing–
Then lull, then leave off. Fury had shrieked "No ling-
Ering! Let me be fell: force I must be brief."

pangs: jabs of pain
schooled at forepangs: taught by the pain which has gone before

wince: flinch with pain

fell: terrible, ruthless
force: perforce, by necessity

O the mind, mind has mountains; cliffs of fall
Frightful, sheer, no-man-fathomed. Hold them cheap   10
May who ne'er hung there. Nor does long our small
Durance deal with that steep or deep. Here! creep,
Wretch, under a comfort serves in a whirlwind: all
Life death does end and each day dies with sleep.

fathomed: measured, understood

durance: endurance, strength

The pride of fickle fortune spareth none,
And, like the floods of swift Enripus borne,
Oft casteth mighty princes from their throne,
And oft the abject captive doth adorn.
She cares not for the wretch's tears and moan,
And the sad groans, which she hath caused, doth scorn.

(Boethius: *fifth century*, translated from Latin)

Thinking/Talking Points

- Try to put the opening *sentence* precisely into your own words.
- What is the dramatic effect of this abrupt beginning? What does the opening suggest to you about the speaker's experiences? (Think about Edgar's reflections.) In what tone of voice would you read it?
- Pick out all the words in the poem which suggest physical or mental pain.
- How many different meanings can you think of for the word "pitch"? Discuss which of them could be working in the phrase: "Pitched past pitch of grief..."
- Why do you think the speaker repeats the word "where" in line 3?
- What pictures of cattle do the words "heave..herds long..huddle" suggest to you? What aspects of grief do these images evoke for you?
- According to the speaker, how is the way Fury works on a person different from the operation of Grief? Which experience do you think is worse? Why?
- What positive human experiences does the phrase "the mind, mind has mountains" suggest to you?
- Suggest why Hopkins set out these lines as he did:

            cliffs of fall
    Frightful, sheer

- How would you describe the rhyme-scheme of Hopkins's sonnet? (See the note on sonnet form on page 118.)
- Discuss the way Hopkins has organised his material within the tight structure of the sonnet. What do you think are the advantages and disadvantages of exploring such powerful feelings in such a tightly-organised form?

Assignments

Choose one: two hours

- ☐ Using the structure of Hopkins's poem as a model, write a sonnet describing a moment of high emotion using imagery usually associated with physical activity, for example:
  —falling in love in terms of walking through s summer meadow
  —hatred in terms of demolishing a bulding.

- ☐ Examine the way in which Hopkins communicates the experience of mental anguish through images of physical suffering in "No

Worst, There is None". What do you find most and least effective about the way he writes?

☐ Discuss the ways in which the form of this poem determines its dramatic impact. (Talk about the use of punctuation, rhyme and lineation as well as the way Hopkins has used the limits imposed by sonnet form.

A Note on Sonnet Form

The sonnet form was introduced into England from Italy in the sixteenth century. Most English sonnets have fourteen lines. Many poets have been attracted to writing in this form because it is so demanding. How can anyone pack all s/he has to say into so few lines? You may like to look at the very different ways Donne, Milton and Wilfred Owen have exploited the sonnet form.

Various sonnet rhyme-schemes have been used. Shakespeare uses the form of four quatrains (each rhyming abab) followed by a rhyming couplet. See if you can describe the form of Hopkins's sonnet.

There are various ways of exploiting the sonnet's tight, fourteen-line structure. Frequently, as in the case of "No Worst, There Is None" the poem falls into two unequal halves: the *octave* (the first eight lines) being answered or balanced by the *sestet* (the last six lines).

Thom Gunn

HUMAN CONDITION

Read this poem carefully a few times.

Human Condition

Now it is fog, I walk
Contained within my coat;
No castle more cut off
By reason of its moat:
Only the sentry's cough,   5
The mercenaries' talk.

The street lamps, visible,
Drop no light on the ground,
But press beams painfully
In a yard of fog around.   10
I am condemned to be
An individual.

In the established border
There balances a mere
Pinpoint of consciousness.   15
I stay, or start from, here:
No fog makes more or less
The neighbouring disorder.

Particular, I must
Find out the limitation   20
Of mind and universe,
To pick thought and sensation
And turn to my own use
Disordered hate or lust.

I seek, to break, my span.   25
I am my one touchstone.

"A Handful of Dust" by Mandy Millbank, a year thirteen student.

This is a test more hard
Than any ever known.
And thus I keep my guard
On that which makes me man.   30

Much is unknowable.
No problem shall be faced
Until the problem is;
I, born to fog, to waste,
Walk through hypothesis,   35
An individual.

First Assignment

Two hours

☐ With close attention to the way the ideas are presented, examine the picture of the "Human Condition" Thom Gunn paints in his poem.

Second Assignment

In pairs: one hour

☐ There are two students' responses to the assignment you have tackled on pages 165 and 167. Can you agree what is good or bad about them? Draft a page or so of critical comments addressed to the writers of each of the essays, commenting in some detail on what you think are the strengths and weaknesses of their responses.

John Donne and Angela Carter

ELEGY XIX (1598)

and from

THE MAGIC TOYSHOP (1981)

Elegy XIX

Come, Madam, come, all rest my powers defy,
Until I labour, I in labour lie.
The foe oft-times having the foe in sight,
Is tired with standing though they never fight.
Off with that girdle, like heaven's zone glistering,
But a far fairer world encompassing.
Unpin that spangled breastplate which you wear,
That the eyes of busy fools may be stopped there.
Unlace yourself, for that harmonious chime
Tells me from you, that now 'tis your bed time.
Off with that happy busk, which I envy,
That still can be, and still can stand so nigh.
Your gown going off, such beauteous state reveals,
As when from flowery meads the hill's shadow steals.
Off with that wiry coronet and show
The hairy diadem which on you doth grow;
Now off with those shoes, and then safely tread
In this love's hallowed temple, this soft bed.
In such white robes, heaven's angels used to be
Received by men; thou angel bring'st with thee
A heaven like Mahomet's paradise; and though
Ill spirits walk in white, we easily know
By this these angels from an evil sprite,
Those set out hairs, but these our flesh upright.

Licence my roving hands, and let them go,
Before, behind, between, above, below.
O my America, my new found land,
My kingdom, safeliest when with one man manned,
My mine of precious stones, my empery,
How blessed am I in this discovering thee!
To enter in these bonds, is to be free;
Then where my hand is set, my seal shall be.

Full nakedness, all joys are due to thee,
As souls unbodied, bodies unclothed must be,
To taste whole joys. Gems which you women use
Are like Atlanta's balls, cast in men's views,
That when a fool's eye lighteth on a gem,
His earthly soul may covet theirs, not them.
Like pictures, or like books' gay coverings made
For laymen, are all women thus arrayed;
Themselves are mystic books, which only we
Whom their imputed grace will dignify
Must see revealed. Then since I may know,
As liberally, as to a midwife, show
Thyself: cast all, yea, this white linen hence,
Here is no penance, much less innocence.

To teach thee, I am naked first, why then
What needst thou have more covering than a man.

Thinking/Talking Points

- Discuss the words and phrases which you feel establish the speaker's tone of voice at various moments in the poem. Experiment with reading the poem out loud. Can you agree on how fast, how loudly or softly it should be spoken?
- How would you describe the speaker's feelings towards the woman he is speaking to?
- What impression of the woman does the poem give you? Which details are responsible for this impression? What is the effect of not hearing her speak?

First Assignment

Two hours

☐ When you have discussed the poem in detail, read through the following two views of the piece and discuss which (if either) you find the more persuasive "reading" of Donne's "Elegy XIX".

A

It was considered too indecent to print and was omitted from the first edition of Donne's poems... in 1633.

The despotic lover... ordering his submissive girl-victim to strip and drawing attention to his massive erection... a perennial dweller in the shadow land of pornography, particularly attractive as a fantasy role to males who... find relations with women difficult...

Emphasis is placed on the richness of the woman's clothes... The luscious sex-symbol whom Donne puts through her paces may be... an aristocrat... In these respects the situation Donne has concocted gratifies not only his sexual but also his social and financial ambitions. The luxurious accessories in his fantasies seem as important to him as the strip-tease itself...

More important than either is the urge to dominate... he contrives to sound... high-minded and dissolute at the same time...

His contempt extends not only to his mesmerised victim but to large sections of the human race... The poem's climax is a general eulogy of nakedness, not... an inventory of this particular girl's anatomical assets. Indeed, it comes as something of a surprise, given the elegy's... general air of lust, to realise that it does not start to mention any part of the girl's body except her hair – not so much as a lip or toe nail, let alone a breast or a thigh. The salivating survey of female physique... de rigueur in most Elizabethan pornography (see, for instance, Thomas Nashe's enjoyable "the Choice of Valentines") has vanished... Donne is rarified and abstracted. He hardly seems to see the girl... his appraising eye dwells on the clothes she takes off... He can feel that he has scaled the pinnacle of wordly, as well as erotic, success, and is not lover but ruler. A "kingdom" and "Empiree" are at his command, in bed.

from John Carey: *John Donne, Life, Mind and Art* (1981)

B

The significant thing about Carey's comments is that he fails to relate many of them to any textual detail. He asserts the tone is hectoring, obscene, salacious but does the text support that reading?

Maybe he suffers from the sexual immaturity he charges Donne with? Does he fall into the trap of believing a woman taking off her clothes can only be titillating, that a man watching her do that can only be a voyeur?

Is this like a commentary on a peep-show?

Your gown's going off, such beauteous state reveals,
As when from flowery meads the hill's shadow steals.

Or is it a delicate, sensitive appreciation of something supremely beautiful? Is it just his own sexual ache and need for its relief which the speaker is worked up about or is it the woman's beauty, the beauty of sex itself and the prospect of their making love together which he is celebrating?

No one would deny it is an erotic poem; but perhaps its an Anglo-Saxon Puritanism which thinks that must mean it is therefore dirty, smutty, something to giggle about rather than embrace as an expression of supreme human happiness; I can't help feeling that Carey is the grubby-minded thirteen year-old, not Donne. Will you deny that naked-ness and making love is or can be utterly lovely?

It is not a strip-tease controlled by a bullying male since he is naked (therefore vulnerable and with his erection rather ridiculous) first.

> then safely tread
> In this love's hallowed temple, this soft bed

Listen to the sound of this: tender, gentle, reverent: not harsh, hectoring or salacious. He's not claiming that making love is a spiritual experience but that it is worthy of reverence, something precious, rare, possibly only to those who value love, prize their sexuality. His attitude reminds me of Lawrence's with its insistance on "tenderness".

The speaker's enjoyment of his lover's body is not the enjoyment of an object which will ease his lust: it is a woman's body which he reveres, explores, enjoys for its own sake:

> Thou angel bring'st with thee
> A heaven like Mahomet's paradise..
>
> O my America, ...
>
> My mine of precious stones..
> How blessed am I in this discovering thee..

He relishes her for her sexual self, not simply to supply his needs: it is her womanhood that he savours, not his own sensations: this feeling is love not lust because it is directed outwards. As he explores her body, he caresses her and reveres her: it is not abusing her body:

> Licence my roving hands....

Notice how the rhythm suggests his tender and slow exploration, delight in each part of her body, culminating in her sex:

```
Behind, before, above, between, below.

Think how her body is like a mine of precious stones.
Think how a woman-hater (a pornographer) would describe that.
It is he, not she who will lose his freedom:

To enter these bonds...

Signing the contract with his sperm is a commitment of his self:

Then where my hand is set, my seal shall be.
Full nakedness, all joys are due to thee.

He emphasises that he is naked as well: full nakedness is their
bodies together - not him drooling over hers from inside a suit of
clothes. The emphasis is upon mutual surrender and togetherness.
```

**(from a response to the extract from John Carey's book by a year thirteen student,
Sam Udwadia)**

Second Assignment

Individual work: two hours

☐ Here is the opening of Angela Carter's novel *The Magic Toyshop*
which was published in 1981. Compare and contrast this passage
with Donne's "Elegy XIX" (published in 1595) in any ways you
find interesting. Refer closely to the texts of both works in your
response.

The summer she was fifteen, Melanie discovered she was made of
flesh and blood. O, my America, my new found land. She embarked
on a tranced voyage, exploring the whole of herself, clambering her
own mountain ranges, penetrating the moist richness of her secret
valleys, a physiological Cortez, da Gama or Mungo Park. For hours
she stared at herself, naked, in the mirror of her wardrobe; she would
follow with her finger the elegant structure of her rib-cage, where the
heart fluttered under the flesh like a bird under a blanket, and she
would draw down the long line from breast-bone to navel (which was
a mysterious cavern or grotto), and she would rasp her palms against
her bud-wing shoulder blades. And then she would writhe about,
clasping herself, laughing sometimes doing cartwheels and handstands
out of sheer exhilaration at the supple surprise of herself now she was
no longer a little girl.

She also posed in attitudes, holding things. Pre-Raphaelite, she combed out her long, black hair to stream, straight down from a centre parting and thoughtfully regarded herself as she held a tiger-lily from the garden under her chin, her knees pressed close together. A la Toulouse Lautrec, she dragged her hair sluttishly across her face and sat down in a chair with her legs apart and a bowl of water and a towel at her feet. She always felt particularly wicked when she posed for Lautrec, although she made up fantasies in which she lived in his time (she had been a chorus-girl or a model and fed a sparrow with crumbs from her Paris attic window). In these fantasies, she helped him and loved him because she was sorry for him, since he was a dwarf and a genius.

She was too thin for a Titian or a Renoir but she contrived a pale, smug Cranach Venus with a bit of net curtain wound round her head and the necklace of cultured pearls they gave her when she was confirmed at her throat. After she read "Lady Chatterley's Lover", she secretly picked forget-me-nots and stuck them in her pubic hair.

Further, she used the net curtain as raw material for a series of nightgowns suitable for her wedding-night which she designed for herself. She gift-wrapped herself for a phantom bridegroom taking a shower and cleaning his teeth in an extra-dimensional bathroom-of-the-future in honeymoon Cannes. Or Venice. Or Miami Beach. She conjured him so intensely to leap the spacetime barrier between them that she could almost feel his breath on her cheek and his voice husking "darling".

In readiness for him, she revealed a long, marbly white leg up to the thigh (forgetting the fantasy in sudden absorption in the mirrored play of muscle as she flexed her leg again and again); then, pulling the net tight, she examined the swathed shape of her small, hard breasts. Their size disappointed her but she supposed they would do.

Edith Wharton

from THE HOUSE OF MIRTH

Assignment

Two hours

☐ This is the opening of Edith Wharton's novel, *The House of Mirth*, which was published in New York in 1905.

Read it through carefully a few times and then write an essay answering the following question:

What impression of Lily Bart and the world she lives in does Edith Wharton give you at the outset of her novel? With close attention to tone, diction, structure and imagery, examine the various ways this impression is created.

(At this stage in the course, we hope you feel confident enough to write about this passage unaided. If you feel you need help, look at the prompt points on page 132.)

Book One

I

Selden paused in surprise. In the afternoon rush of the Grand Central Station his eyes had been refreshed by the sight of Miss Lily Bart.

It was a Monday in early September, and he was returning to his work from a hurried dip into the country; but what was Miss Bart doing in town at that season? If she had appeared to be catching a train, he might have inferred that he had come on her in the act of transition between one and another of the country-houses which disputed her presence after the close of the Newport season; but her desultory air perplexed him. She stood apart from the crowd, letting it drift by her to the platform or the street, and wearing an air of irresolution which might, as he surmised, be the mask of a very definite purpose. It struck him at once that she was waiting for someone, but he hardly knew why the idea arrested him. There was nothing new about Lily Bart, yet he could never see her without a faint movement of interest: it was characteristic of her that she always roused speculation, that her simplest acts seemed the result of far-reaching intentions.

An impulse of curiosity made him turn out of his direct line to the door, and stroll past her. He knew that if she did not wish to be seen she would contrive to elude him; and it amused him to think of putting her skill to the test.

"Mr Selden—what good luck!"

She came forward smiling, eager almost, in her resolve to intercept him. One or two persons, in brushing past them, lingered to look; for Miss Bart was a figure to arrest even the suburban traveller rushing to his last train.

Selden had never seen her more radiant. Her vivid head, relieved against the dull tints of the crowd, made her more conspicuous than in a ball-room, and under her dark hat and veil she regained the girlish smoothness, the purity of tint, that she was beginning to lose after eleven years of late hours and indefatigable dancing. Was it really eleven years, Selden found himself wondering, and had she indeed reached the nine-and-twentieth birthday with which her rivals credited her?

"What luck!" she repeated. "How nice of you to come to my rescue!"

He responded joyfully that to do so was his mission in life, and asked what form the rescue was to take.

"Oh, almost any—even to sitting on a bench and talking to me. One sits out a cotillion—why not sit out a train? It isn't a bit hotter here than in Mrs Van Osburgh's conservatory—and some of the women are not a bit uglier."

She broke off, laughing, to explain that she had come up to town from Tuxedo, on her way to the Gus Trenors' at Bellomont, and had missed the three-fifteen train to Rhinebeck.

"And there isn't another till half-past five." She consulted the little jewelled watch among her laces. "Just two hours to wait. And I don't know what to do with myself. My maid came up this morning to do some shopping for me, and was to go on to Bellomont at one o'clock, and my aunt's house is closed, and I don't know a soul in town." She glanced plaintively about the station. "It *is* hotter than Mrs Van Osburgh's, after all. If you can spare the time, do take me somewhere for a breath of air."

He declared himself entirely at her disposal: the adventure struck him as diverting. As a spectator, he had always enjoyed Lily Bart; and his course lay so far out of her orbit that it amused him to be drawn for a moment into the sudden intimacy which her proposal implied.

"Shall we go over to Sherry's for a cup of tea?"

She smiled assentingly, and then made a slight grimace.

"So many people come up to town on a Monday—one is sure to meet a lot of bores. I'm as old as the hills, of course, and it ought not

to make any difference; but if *I'm* old enough, you're not," she
objected gaily. "I'm dying for tea—but isn't there a quieter place?"

He answered her smile, which rested on him vividly. Her discretion
interested him almost as much as her imprudences: he was so sure
that both were part of the same carefully-elaborated plan. In judging
Miss Bart, he had always made use of the "argument from design".

"The resources of New York are rather meagre," he said, "but I'll
find a hansom first, and then we'll invent something."

He led her through the throng of returning holiday-makers, past
sallow-faced girls in preposterous hats, and flat-chested women struggling with paper bundles and palm-leaf fans. Was it possible that she
belonged to the same race? The dinginess, the crudity of this average
section of womanhood made him feel how highly specialized she was.

A rapid shower had cooled the air, and clouds still hung refresh-
ingly over the moist street.

"How delicious! Let us walk a little," she said as they emerged from
the station.

They turned into Madison Avenue and began to stroll northward.
As she moved beside him, with her long light step, Selden was
conscious of taking a luxurious pleasure in her nearness: in the
modelling of her little ear, the crisp upward wave of her hair—was it
ever so lightly brightened by art?—and the thick planting of her
straight black lashes. Everything about her was at once vigorous and
exquisite, at once strong and fine. He had a confused sense that she
must have cost a great deal to make, that a great many dull and ugly
people must, in some mysterious way, have been sacrificed to produce
her. He was aware that the qualities distinguishing her from the herd
of her sex were chiefly external: as though a fine glaze of beauty and
fastidiousness had been applied to vulgar clay. Yet the analogy left
him unsatisfied, for a coarse texture will not take a high finish; and
was it not possible that the material was fine, but that circumstance
had fashioned it into a futile shape?

As he reached this point in his speculations the sun came out, and
her lifted parasol cut off his enjoyment. A moment or two later she
paused with a sigh.

"Oh dear, I'm so hot and thirsty—and what a hideous place New
York is!" She looked despairingly up and down the dreary thorough-
fare. "Other cities put on their best clothes in summer, but New York
seems to sit in its shirt-sleeves." Her eyes wandered down one of the
side-streets. "Some one has had the humanity to plant a few trees
over there. Let us go into the shade."

"I am glad my street meets with your approval," said Selden as they
turned the corner.

"Your street? Do you live here?"

She glanced with interest along the new brick and limestone

house-fronts, fantastically varied in obedience to the American craving for novelty, but fresh and inviting with their awnings and flower-boxes.

"Ah, yes—to be sure: *The Benedick*. What a nice looking building! I don't think I have ever seen it before." She looked across at the flat-house with its marble porch and pseudo-Georgian facade. "Which are your windows? Those with the awnings down?"

"On the top floor—yes."

"And that nice little balcony is yours? How cool it looks up there!"

He paused a moment. "Come up and see," he suggested. "I can give you a cup of tea in no time—and you won't meet any bores."

Her colour deepened—she still had the art of blushing at the right time—but she took the suggestion as lightly as it was made.

"Why not? It's too tempting—I'll take the risk," she declared.

"Oh, I'm not dangerous," he said in the same key. In truth, he had never liked her as well as at that moment. He knew she had accepted without afterthought: he could never be a factor in her calculations, and there was a surprise, a refreshment almost, in the spontaneity of her consent.

On the threshold he paused a moment, feeling for his latch-key.

"There's no one here; but I have a servant who is supposed to come in the mornings, and it's just possible he may have put out the tea-things and provided some cake."

He ushered her into a slip of a hall hung with old prints. She noticed the letters and notes heaped on the table among his gloves and sticks; then she found herself in a small library, dark but cheerful, with its walls of books, a pleasantly faded Turkey rug, a littered desk, and, as he foretold, a tea-tray on a low table near the window. A breeze had sprung up, swaying inward the muslin curtains, and bringing a fresh scent of mignonette and petunias from the flower-box on the balcony.

Lily sank with a sigh into one of the shabby leather chairs.

"How delicious to have a place like this all to one's self! What a miserable thing it is to be a woman!" She leaned back in a luxury of discontent.

Selden was rummaging in a cupboard for the cake.

"Even women," he said, "have been known to enjoy the privileges of a flat."

"Oh, governesses—or widows. But not girls—not poor, miserable, marriageable girls!"

"I even know a girl who lives in a flat."

She sat up in surprise. "You do?"

"I do," he assured her, emerging from the cupboard with the sought-for cake.

"Oh, I know—you mean Gerty Farish." She smiled a little

unkindly. "But I said *marriageable*—and besides, she has a horrid little place, and no maid, and such queer things to eat. Her cook does the washing and the food tastes of soap. I should hate that, you know."

"You shouldn't dine with her on wash-days," said Selden, cutting the cake.

They both laughed, and he knelt by the table to light the lamp under the kettle, while she measured out the tea into a little tea-pot of green glaze. As he watched her hand, polished as a bit of old ivory, with its slender pink nails, and the sapphire bracelet slipping over her wrist, he was struck with the irony of suggesting to her such a life as his cousin Gertrude Farish had chosen. She was so evidently the victim of the civilization which had produced her, that the links of her bracelet seemed like manacles chaining her to her fate.

Prompt Points

- Jot down your immediate feelings about Lily after reading this chapter. Which words would you use to describe her? Would you choose any of these?

strong	wayward	lonely	enticing	captive
magnetic	brave	coy	modest	poised
mysterious	frank	devious	energetic	proud

Add some words of your own.
- What words would you use to describe Selden? Are they similar or different from the ones you chose to describe Lily? Why is this the case?
- How significant do you feel Lily's *gender* is in the way she speaks and behaves in this chapter? To what extent do you feel the writer expects the reader to be aware of gender as an issue here? On what evidence?
- Do you think Lily comes from a particular *social class?* If so, which details suggest that? To what extent do you feel her social class controls the way she speaks and behaves? Which details help you to make up your mind about this?
- What details in the extract bring out the differences between New York society in the 1890s and the one in which you live?
- What strikes you as unusual or interesting about the way Edith Wharton *presents* Selden and Lily Bart?
- Pick out what you think are the dozen or so most important quotations to use in answering the assignment question. Do these quotations pick out what is interesting about Wharton's style as well as the information she conveys?
- What do you think Edith Wharton's purposes may have been in this opening chapter? What predictions would you make about the way the novel may develop?

Henry James

from WHAT MAISIE KNEW

What Maisie Knew was published in 1897. It is the story of a young girl whose rich and worthless parents divorce, leaving their daughter to grow up as she will in the most trying of circumstances.

Maisie's situation is described in the following *preamble* to the novel. Read it through carefully *a few times* before considering the questions which follow.

The litigation had seemed interminable and had in fact been complicated; but by the decision on the appeal the judgement of the divorce-court was confirmed as to the assignment of the child. The father, who, though bespattered from head to foot, had made good his case, was, in pursuance of this triumph, appointed to keep her: it was not so much that the mother's character had been more absolutely damaged as that the brilliancy of a lady's complexion (and this lady's, in court, was immensely remarked) might be more regarded as showing the spots. Attached, however, to the second pronouncement was a condition that detracted, for Beale Farange, from its sweet-ness—an order that he should refund to his late wife the twenty-six hundred pounds put down by her, as it was called, some three years before, in the interest of the child's maintenance and precisely on a proved understanding that he would take no proceedings: a sum of which he had had the administration and of which he could render not the least account. The obligation thus attributed to her adversary was no small balm to Ida's resentment; it drew a part of the sting from her defeat and compelled Mr Farange perceptibly to lower his crest. He was unable to produce the money or to raise it in any way; so that after a squabble scarcely less public and scarcely more decent than the original shock of battle his only issue from his predicament was a compromise proposed by his legal advisers and finally accepted by hers.

His debt was by this arrangement remitted to him and the little girl disposed of in a manner worthy of the judgement-seat of Solomon. She was divided in two and the portions tossed impartially to the disputants. They would take her, in rotation, for six months at a time;

she would spend half the year with each. This was odd justice in the eyes of those who still blinked in the fierce light projected from the tribunal—a light in which neither parent figured in the least as a happy example to youth and innocence. What was to have been expected on the evidence was the nomination, *in loco parentis*, of some proper third person, some respectable or at least some presentable friend. Apparently, however, the circle of the Faranges had been scanned in vain for any such ornament; so that the only solution finally meeting all the difficulties was, save that of sending Maisie to a Home, the partition of the tutelary office in the manner I have mentioned. There were more reasons for her parents to agree to it than there had been for them to agree to anything; and they now prepared with her help to enjoy the distinction that waits upon vulgarity sufficiently attested. Their rupture had resounded, and after being perfectly insignificant together they would be decidedly striking apart. Had they not produced an impression that warranted people in looking for appeals in the newspapers for the rescue of the little one-reverberation, amid a vociferous public, of the idea that some movement should be started or some benevolent person should come forward? A good lady came indeed a step or two: she was distantly related to Mrs Farange, to whom she proposed that, having children and nurseries wound up and going, she should be allowed to take home the bone of contention and, by working it into her system, relieve at least one of the parents. This would make every time, for Maisie, after her inevitable six months with Beale, much more of a change.

"More of a change?" Ida cried. "Won't it be enough of a change for her to come from that low brute to the person in the world who detests him most?"

"No, because you detest him so much that you'll always talk to her about him. You'll keep him before her by perpetually abusing him."

Mrs Farange stared. "Pray, then, am I to do nothing to counteract his villainous abuse of me?"

The good lady, for a moment, made no reply: her silence was a grim judgement of the whole point of view. "Poor little monkey!" she at last exclaimed; and the words were an epitaph for the tomb of Maisie"s childhood. She was abandoned to her fate. What was clear to any spectator was that the only link binding her to either parent was this lamentable fact of her being a ready vessel for bitterness, a deep little porcelain cup in which biting acids could be mixed. They had wanted her not for any good they could do her, but for the harm they could, with her unconscious aid, do each other. She should serve their anger and seal their revenge, for husband and wife had been alike crippled by the heavy hand of justice, which in the last resort met on neither side their indignant claim to get, as they called it, everything.

If each was only to get half this seemed to concede that neither was so base as the other pretended, or, to put it differently, offered them both as bad indeed, since they were only as good as each other. The mother had wished to prevent the father from, as she said, "so much as looking" at the child; the father's plea was that the mother's lightest touch was "simply contamination". These were the opposed principles in which Maisie was to be educated—she was to fit them together as she might. Nothing could have been more touching at first than her failure to suspect the ordeal that awaited her little unspotted soul. There were persons horrified to think what those in charge of it would combine to try to make of it: no one could conceive in advance that they would be able to make nothing ill.

This was a society in which for the most part people were occupied only with chatter, but the disunited couple had at last grounds for expecting a time of high activity. They girded their loins, they felt as if the quarrel had only begun. They felt indeed more married than ever, inasmuch as what marriage had mainly suggested to them was the unbroken opportunity to quarrel. There had been "sides" before, and there were sides as much as ever; for the sider too the prospect opened out, taking the pleasant form of a superabundance of matter for desultory conversation. The many friends of the Faranges drew together to differ about them; contradiction grew young again over teacups and cigars. Everybody was always assuring everybody of something very shocking, and nobody would have been jolly if nobody had been outrageous. The pair appeared to have a social attraction which failed merely as regards each other: it was indeed a great deal to be able to say for Ida that no one but Beale desired her blood, and for Beale that if he should ever have his eyes scratched out it would be only by his wife. It was generally felt, to begin with, that they were awfully good-looking—they had really not been analysed to a deeper residuum. They made up together, for instance, some twelve feet three of stature, and nothing was more discussed than the apportionment of this quantity. The sole flaw in Ida's beauty was a length and reach of arm conducive perhaps to her having so often beaten her ex-husband at billiards, a game in which she showed a superiority largely accountable, as she maintained, for the resentment finding expression in his physical violence. Billiards was her great accomplishment and the distinction her name always first produced the mention of. Notwithstanding some very long lines everything about her that might have been large and that in many women profited by the licence was, with a single exception, admired and cited for its smallness. The exception was her eyes, which might have been of mere regulation size, but which overstepped the modesty of nature; her mouth, on the other hand, was barely perceptible, and odds were freely taken as to the measurement of her waist. She was a person who, when she was out—and she was always out—produced everywhere a sense of having been seen often, the sense indeed of a kind of abuse of visibility, so that it would have been, in the usual places, rather vulgar to wonder at her. Strangers only did that; but they, to the amusement of the familiar, did it very much: it was an inevitable way of betraying an alien habit. Like her husband she carried clothes, carried them as a train carries passengers: people had been known to compare their taste and dispute about the accommodation they gave these articles, though inclining on the whole to the commendation of Ida as less overcrowded, especially with jewellery and flowers. Beale Farange had natural decorations, a kind of costume in his vast fair beard, burnished like a gold breastplate, and in the eternal glitter of the teeth that his long moustache had been trained not to hide and that gave him, in every possible situation, the look of the joy of life. He had been destined in his youth for diplomacy and momentarily attached, without a salary, to a legation which enabled him often to say, "In *my* time in the East": but contemporary history had somehow had no use for him, had hurried past him and left him in perpetual Piccadilly. Every one knew what he had—only twenty-five hundred. Poor Ida, who had run through everything, had now nothing but her carriage and her paralysed uncle. This old brute, as he was called, was supposed to have a lot put away. The child was provided for, thanks to a crafty godmother, a defunct aunt of Beale's, who had left her something in such a manner that the parent's could appropriate only the income.

Thinking/Talking Points

- Discuss your initial reactions to the way Henry James writes. What makes his writing different from what you have read in this volume of Dickens's prose (see page 82) for example, or D H Lawrence's (see page 24)? How is his writing like or unlike Edith Wharton's (see page 128)?
  You may like to consider the following aspects of James's style:
  (a) his diction
  (b) his sentence and paragraph structure
  (c) his tone
  (d) his use of imagery
  (e) his expectations of the reader.
- Work out:
  (a) why, initially, Beale was given custody of Maisie by the court
  (b) why Beale had to compromise
  (c) what compromise arrangement the court decided upon
  (d) what suggestion the "good lady" made to benefit Maisie

(e) why Maisie's mother declined her offer

(f) why Maisie's parents were so determined to hang on to their share of Maisie's custody

(g) who had "provided for" Maisie and what was shrewd about the way she did it

(h) what (i) Beale and (ii) Ida looked like.

- Pick out a dozen or so details from the preamble which give you an impression of the kind of world the Faranges live in, the sort of people who are their friends and acquaintances.

- The narrator describes Maisie, using a very striking image, as "a ready vessel for bitterness, a deep little porcelain cup in which biting acids could be mixed".

  Describe the various thoughts and feelings this image conjures up for you.

- Why, after their divorce, do the Faranges feel "more married than ever"?

- Make a balance sheet of "strengths" and "shortcomings" for Ida and for Beale. Do you feel the narrator presents the couple as equally praise/blame worthy or do you find one more sympathetically presented than the other? Supply the evidence.

- From all that we are given in the preamble, how would you expect Maisie's future to develop?

- The situation Maisie finds herself in is described to us by an *omniscient narrator*: the person telling the story knows everything. Do you get the impression that the narrator has any feelings about what s/he describes so carefully or is s/he totally detached and impartial? Pick out some phrases to support your opinion.

Assignments

Choose one: two hours

☐ Write an essay in which you explore what you take to be the purpose of the preamble to James's novel *What Maisie Knew*. Describe some of the techniques James uses to achieve the effects he does.

☐ Read through the two sample responses to this question on page 170. Discuss the ways the students have gone about answering the question. Write a critical commentary on what each has written, referring closely to James's text.

Sample Student Responses

Johnson's style

Write a passage of about one hundred words of your own, comparing and contrasting any city with any village you know, imitating features of Johnson's style. Then write a commentary on what you have produced, describing the ways in which your piece is similar to/different from his.

If there are two place most unlike, then, after consideration, these are they.

One is full of mess if full of life, the other clean but comparatively deserted. In London people sweat and rush, in Edale people flow.

The hectic existence of Londoners produces panic and pain; the gentle rhythms of life in Edale hands them freedom from care. London is shops and high streets, Edale is lanes and hills. If they are both in Britain then they feel as if they were on different planets. People may eke out a living in London but people will thrive in Edale.

I have tried to make my passage as like Dr Johnson's as I can. His piece is typical of its period - the C18th - with its careful attention to achieving balance, keeping every sentence and paragraph as symmetrical as possible : the characteristics we see in the formal architecture of the period. Whenever he makes a remark about Dryden, he carefully balances it with a comment on Pope:

Dryden is read with frequent astonishment, and Pope with perpetual delight.

I have tried to parody this balance by talking about Edale immediately after London. I have not attempted to mimic any particular lines from Dr Johnson's passage but his way of using rhythm, tone, tempo and form to create the desired mood of "reasonableness". Although I have not mimicked particular lines I have tried to copy his diction. For example, I think that a key phrase in the original is "with some hesitation". I used "after consideration", to simulate his way of proceeding soundly and with careful judgement.

I have mimicked Dr Johnson's style but he would certainly not agree with the content of my piece. Although he might like the regularity of the rhythm his "the man who is tired of London is tired of life" attitude is contradicted in my passage. I say that people can exist or "eke out a living" in London whereas people only "thrive" away from the noisy city. My passage suggests that peple have a far richer life in Edale than those who inhabit the city. My Londoners are "tired" of it already.

Another phrase of Johnson's that I have mimicked is "The dilatory caution of Pope enabled him to..." I have written "The gentle rhythms of life in Edale hands them... I think "enabled him" is similar to "hands them": both more powerful words than "lets" or "gives".

I think that all in all my passage is quie similar to some of the features of Johnson's style. It has the balanced opposites, symmetry and controlled tone of the original though I have failed to produce a phrase as beautifully crafted as:

> Dryden is read wth frequent astonishment, and Pope with perpetual delight.

Michael Cowland, a year twelve student

D H Lawrence: "Odour of Chrysanthemums"

Write a study of the opening of "Odour of Chrysanthemums", commenting in detail on the way Lawrence's language creates a particular atmosphere and raises certain expectations.

The pit bank loomed up beyond the pond, flames like red sores licking its ashy sides, in the afternoon's stagnant light.

This quotation, with all its bleak, desolate, almost hellish imagery summarises perfectly the beginning of one of Lawrence's most famous short stories "Odour of Chrysanthemums". Even the title does little to instill pleasure and happiness; flowers are fragrant, they do not usually give off an odour. We think of odours as unpleasant smells and chrysanthemums are funeral flowers; in some countries, for example Germany, it is considered a great insult to be given them because it implies that you are soon to die.

Lawrence was a fine artist as well as a writer and he combines these disciplines by painting remarkable and vivid pictures in words. The tone of the extract is industrial, inevitable and thoroughly unappealing from start to finish.

> The small locomotive engine, Number 4, came clanking, stumbling down from Selston with seven full waggons. It appeared round the corner with loud threats of speed...

So much has been written through the years about the romantic quality of the steam train and to this day thousands of enthusiasts all over the world lament its demise and yet here we are presented with an utterly inhuman, unfriendly machine that does not "chug" or "roll" merrily down the track but instead "clanks" and "stumbles" as if only just under the control of its human driver. It gives "loud threats of speed" but is not travelling particularly swiftly as a colt "outdistanced it at a canter".

Lawrence impresses upon us that this train with its "seven full wagons" could quite easily go a lot faster as it travels through the "gorse"; a brambly, prickly unwelcoming hedge.

The domination of the people by machinery since the Industrial Revolution is emphasised symbolically as a lone, seemingly vulnerable woman has to draw back into the hedge and "watched the footplate advancing".

> The trucks thumped heavily past, one by one, with slow inevitable movement, as she stood, insignificantly trapped between the jolting black waggons and the hedge...

A tangible rhythm emerges in this extract as we imagine the "black waggons" as they "thumped heavily past, one by one". The woman is "insignif-icantly trapped" between foul, dirty "black waggons" and the brambly, prickly hedge. In a sense, she is surrounded.

The train continues on its relentless way, "towards the coppice where the withered oak leaves dropped noiselessly...". There is a sense that the landscape has been blighted by the onset of industry making the oak leaves "withered". The word "withered" is normally associated with old age and decay. The fields are "dreary and forsaken", perhaps abandoned because they simply could not sustain a crop any more; their soils polluted with dust and grime and other unnatural, infertile menaces.

There is a "reedy pit-pond...abandoned by the fowls" and presumably devoid of any life. Lawrence does not need to go into any more detail; we can imagine exactly how it looks: cold and unwelcoming and full of thick, murky water, empty besides the odd struggling reed that somehow manages to keep itself above water.

The deserting birds now live in "the tarred fowl-house". Yet more horrible, suffocating dirt is described, a dirt that can cover whole houses and which no one can escape from. It may not be able to invade the interiors of these houses, but its mark can be seen everywhere else, infecting the environment with a dark, evil tinge that surely must have an effect on everyone living in it.

> The pit bank loomed up beyond the pond, flames like red sores
> licking its ashy sides, in the afternoon's stagnant light.

The pit bank is the dominating feature of the landscape, looming over Underwood "in the afternoon's stagnant light". How can light be described as "stagnant" unless it is exactly that: stale, sluggish, or dull from inaction. Perhaps the sunlight is filtered by the pit dust floating in the air, making one day monotonously similar to the next. "Flames like red sores...licking...its ashy sides". Fire and pain and dust and dirt are all apparent once again and one can only compare these unsavoury elements to Hell.

The mine itself sounds grubby and unpleasant with its "tapering chimneys and the clumsy, black headstocks of Brinsley Colliery". Like the waggons of the train, the headstocks are black with dirt and Lawrence does not let us forget that.

And then suddenly, unobtrusively, we are told in one short sentence that "the miners were being turned up". After describing in intricate detail the machinery and the environment that it has blighted, Lawrence presents the men who work to keep that machinery going apparently with near-contempt or at best, total indifference. One could argue that their insignificance is exaggerated, perhaps also the state of the environment, but one has to remember Lawrence grew up in a typical mining town in Eastwood, Nottinghamshire and he endured everything that this unnatural environment could throw at him throughout his formative years.

The miners, returning at the end of the day from their long, exhausting shifts "passed like shadows diverging home". Reading this description at face value, we would assume they had been called "shadows" because of the dark coal soot that would have covered them from head to foot, blackening every part of their bodies. But these miners could be people resigned to living under the shadow of industry until their dying days and as a result have been drained of humanity and identity and instead drift along as one indistinguishable group, their identities only partially restored after a good bath. There is an almost ghostly quality about them as they make their way back to their blackened homes. Perhaps each day they have had to spend in the mine has gradually eroded those identities that seem lost, hidden deep behind coal soot.

Mrs Bates, the central character in the story is:

A tall woman of imperious mien, handsome, with definite black eyebrows. Her smooth black hair was parted exactly... Her face was calm and set, her mouth was closed with disillusionment.

Lawrence seems to be emphasising that perhaps Mrs Bates is just that bit above the normal folk you would find living in a mining town. She is tall, and of "imperious mien", therefore slightly overbearing and domineering. Typical miners' wives were, in theory at least, obedient mothers who stayed at home with the children and housekeeping to deal with. Mrs Bates seems slightly more than that, with her "smooth black hair...that...was parted exactly". The fact that her mouth is "closed with disillusionmemnt" indicates that hers is a face of sad, painful experience. Perhaps she has lost faith in life, in herself.

The house that herself and her family live in has a bricked yard where a "few wintery primroses" are growing. Once again, Lawrence demonstrates the harshness of the environment, where flowers – normally a symbol of life and beauty – are "wintery". There are also "some twiggy apple trees, winter-crack trees, and ragged cabbages". This garden, whilst managing to sustain some sort of life, emphasises the sordidness and unlovliness of the area. The "ragged cabbages" sound distinctly unappetising, presumably sprouting dry, lifeless leaves and being lightly doused in a fine film of coal soot.

John Bates, her younger son, "a sturdy boy of five" is a casualty of this inexorable progress. He is not a happy, inquisitive and loving boy but is instead "resentful" and "taciturn":

He was dressed in trousers and waistcoat of cloth that was too thick and hard for the size of the garments. They were evidently cut down from a man's clothes.

This is a boy dressed in a man's clothes who is already well on his way to his final destiny, the destiny of every young boy in Underwood: to be a miner just like his father. Whether the boy knows this already is questionable but what is obvious is that he is "defiant" and "resentful". He says nothing in this extract and his actions are tinged with aggression. He tears "at ragged wisps of chrysanthemums and... drops...the petals in handfuls along the path". These petals are later described as "wan", a word which sums up the extract: tired, sad and dreary.

The extract ends with the train "looming" past the house and coming to a stop outside the gate. The two main elements of this extract: the Number 4 steam train and Mrs Bates finally meet and it is surely here that the story begins.

The vividness of the extract as a whole is, at some points, chilling. Lawrence manages to entwine his painting and writing skills to present the reader with a picture of Underwood from every single angle. The unnatural metamorphosis of a once beautiful environment into a blighted, near-lifeless landscape and how people and nature have coped with it is cleverly depicted. Lawrence leaves no stone unturned and as a result, when the story begins, we can immerse ourselves in the twists and turns of the plot more completely than we could with a more conventionally written story.

James Lant, a year twelve student

Amy Lowell: "Spring Day"

Write an appreciation of Amy Lowell's piece from "Spring Day". What do you think she was trying to do? What is distinctive about the way she does it? Select and comment upon eight or nine details which impress you and describe how they achieve their effect.

This passage creates a busy, alive street scene. It could be in any town – it's what we can all imagine quite easily as a town full of shoppers, workers, children. The town has a happy, colourful atmosphere perhaps not so common: maybe life in 1916 had a positive feel to it even though there was a war on!

These impressions created by words like "crowded", "waves of people" are of many people perhaps on their way back from work or on a Saturday. The happy atmosphere is conveyed by the sunshine, blue sky and colour; also by the healthy business of the town with "traffic", "loud bangs", "murmuring out of high windows" "whirling of machine belts" and "blurring of horses".

The movement is emphasised by having the contrast of the "stock-still...old church" in the midst of the "waves of people". The church, chemists and pavement are also solid, steady and not moving; they are important to balance the passage. After all, the town is also the buildings and stationary things.

> Feet tripping, skipping, lagging, dragging plodding doggedly or
> springing up and advancing on firm elastic insteps

I like this part of the passage because it describes so well the different ways different people walk, reflecting their different moods or personalities. Like happy children, tired after a long day, fed up, determined, single minded or carefree. She makes the point that a town is a unit and an individual has little or no importance but the effect is very different from what we had in the passage from "Hard Times". Acceptance rather than misery:

> I am a part of the town, a bit of blown dust thrust along with the
> crowd

Although these people operate as a unit I don't think there can be complete unity between any number of people. This article is impersonal when it talks about people: it talks about "crowds" and "a boy". But even when she mentions the boy the emphasis is on the smell of the newspaper not the child as a person.

On the whole the passage seems to be a bit forced, as though the writer was consciously attempting to write something great:

> The blue sky pales to lemon and great tongues of gold blind the
> shop windows putting out their contents in a flood of flame.

I think she contradicts/confuses images here with the sky "paling to lemon" – a soft, mild colour – but causing the chemist's shop to look like "a flood of flame".

I feel this passage almost manages to create the desired atmosphere but some of the detail is a little ridiculous.

Elizabeth Hargrave, a year twelve student

* * * * *

In this fragment, Lowell recreates the bustling, lively, often bewildering atmosphere of a busy street using varied language to create sharp contrasts of sights, sounds and smells to bring the scene alive.

The piece opens with:

Swirl of crowded streets

Immediately the hectic movement of a busy city street is suggested by the word "swirl". It conjures up the impression of a fast, random swarm of people, moving so swiftly they become just a blur to the eye as you look at them. Then comes the word "shock": short and sharp, having such an impact that it makes the reader sit up and take notice. This is much like the feeling of when you are swept away in a sea of people, then, all of a sudden find yourself at the edge of a busy road. It makes you suddenly jump back and stop.

The detail of the chemists shops:

...with their blue, gold, purple jars, darting colours far into
the crowd

provides a sense of richness to the eye. The variety and splendour of these bold, vivid colours which themselves mingle with the crowd add a wealth of diverse sight. The word "darting" with its strong hard "d" sound followed by a short sharp vowel imitates the action it is describing. I imagine sharp, narrow shafts of intense colour shooting out, almost like missiles, into the street.

Then there follows a series of contrasting sounds to make the reader aware of the wonderful variety, incredible array of noises to be heard and enjoyed in such a situation. There are: "bangs...murmurs...whirling...blurring...shudder...knocking".

The word "bangs" bursts from the mouth like an explosion, whereas "murmurings" with its repetition of the dull "mur" sound is vague and indecipherable, mimicking the low, rambling monotone sound of vague and distant voices. "Whirling" with its long, drawn-out vowel sound suggests the constant motion of "machine belts" pulling themselves round and round. It is difficult to say the word "shudder" without letting the mouth judder slightly, producing on a small scale the effect of the movement the writer has described.

This all has the effect of making the street scene come alive in our

minds; we are forced to imagine that we are experiencing the same sensations
that we would be feeling it we were ourselves in this street.

Lowell does not use "proper" (complete) sentences in this piece. This
makes everything read quickly, giving us the impression of breathless,
instant, on-the-spot reporting. It also enables the sensation to come across
of everything's happening at the same time. All the noises and sights seem
almost to be in battle with one another, fighting for attention. This also
conveys a sense of confusion. The writer states:

> I am a piece of the town, a bit of blown dust thrust along with
> the crowd.

Describing herself as "dust" suggest the insignificance of the individual in the crowd, a loss of identity. She is passive, being "thrust"
along. No longer does she have any control over her movements, she has
become part of something much bigger and more powerful than her own being.
The word "thrust" carries with it the force of the feeling of being pushed
along, unable to resist. The writer does not, however, feel resentment or
panic against this loss of individuality:

> Proud to feel the pavement under me reeling with feet

It is impossible to pronounce the word "proud" without making it sound
bold and upright. The vowel sound forces you to open your mouth wide, giving
the word an air of utter confidence.

Much like the description of various sounds, we are then given a list
of present participles – all the different ways in which people are moving:

> feet tripping, skipping, lagging, dragging, plodding doggedly, or
> springing up...

The words "tripping" and "skipping" both suggest quick, lively movements whereas "dragging" and "lagging" both have long vowel sounds which
slow the pace, imitating the slow tied steps of someone moving his/her feet
reluctantly along the ground. The phrase "doggedly plodding" is steady and
rhythmic, like sure-footed, heavy footsteps moving in time to a constant
rhythm. The word "springing" is uplifting and lively. When said out loud, it
naturally comes out in a light, high-pitched voice.

Having appealed to our senses of touch, sight and hearing, Amy Lowell
then creates in words intense sensations of smell: "Pungent as tulips and
narcissus". The word "pungent" is a strong word, suggesting an intense,

stifling, overbearing smell, just as the scent of flowers mentioned is powerful. I think it is interesting to compare something as ordinary, dirty and grey as a newspaper with bright, fresh, natural flowers: it's characteristic of this writer's love of the city and of being alive.

The last sentence provides a beautiful image of the sun lowering in the sky and piercing the windows of the shops:

great tongues of gold blind the shop-windows

"Great" suggests something splendid and over-awing. The colour of gold is rich and warm. The image is heavenly. In biblical passages God is often spoken of an manifesting himself in great tongues of fire. This is something wonderful, beautiful and mysterious sent from the skies.

The passage ends:

in a flood of flame

"Flood" suggests something dramatic and overwhelming. As well as making it forceful and dramatic, the alliteration here also provides a musically satisfying ending.

I think that in this short piece Amy Lowell has managed to evoke in my mind all the colour, bustle, excitement, confusion, noise and movement of a bust street by using many contrasting and colourful sounds and words to bring the scene alive.

Karen Marie Smith, a year twelve student

Joyce Grenfell: "Sing-Song Time"

Here is the opening to a short story. Read it through and note distinctive elements of tone, diction and style. Then write three or four more paragraphs continuing the story in a suitable manner.

Write a commentary describing the features of the original which you have tried to emulate, and assessing your degree of success.

Well, try imagining what it would be like to be a fish.
No Sarah, we're not doing drama today.
I'm sure you would be a lovely fish, but we're singing today.
Because today's Monday.
Yes, I know we have actions to our song.
No, that's not the same as drama. So, shall we start our Drum Marching

Song? We don't have any drums in our classroom, so we'll clap our hands instead.

Not too hard Jacqueline, or you'll hurt yourself.

Very good James, the dustbin is like a drum.

No! Sidney!

I did NOT suggest that you tried it out.

It's not funny or clever children, so we don't laugh at him.

Now, pick up the bits of paper, Sidney, and come and sit back down.

Sit next to me, down here.

Of course Sidney isn't my favourite, David.

No, there's not room for both of you to sit here.

I mind.

Thank you Sidney. One can almost forgive them anything when they try so hard to join in, can't one, Mrs Boulting?

Now, surely someone can remember how our Drum Marching Song begins?

Thank you Caroline.

Thank you Caroline.

Caroline...

I think we'd better let everyone else join in now, Caroline.

Caroline!

Thank you Miss Boulting.

Because she played the piano for us.

I know it's her job.

But we're being kind to each other today, and it doesn't hurt to say "thank you". Does anyone remember the name of the song we sang last week?

Children, you know we don't shout out in our classroom.

That's right Susan, it's in our class rules.

Yes, David?

No, not "Twinkle, Twinkle Little Star."

There is no narrative in this piece, no stage directions, no spoken description. In fact, all we get is one side of a fairly complex conversation. Yet it is very easy to picture exactly what is going on. We are told, directly, the place, – a "classroom", the time of day "time to start our day's work". All the other details are built up, most significantly through the speaker's tone of voice and diction. I think the writer assumes we will remember a day like this from our lives, and by presenting it only by the teacher's voice allows us to develop our own picture.

The speaker uses "us" and "our" all the time, trying to bridge the gap between her authority and the children:

Children, we've had our run .... now it's time to start our day's
work

This attempt at equality on the speaker's part first makes us more
aware of how different the writer thinks the two groups really are. The
thought of this teacher having had a "run" is ridiculous. Despite the
feeling that she is trying so hard to avoid it, I find the speaker patron-
ising. The differentiation between "us" and "them" is enhanced by the use of
italics:

He's rather disruptive ... encouraged, bless his heart.

The affection the speaker feels for these children comes through her
patient treatment of the disruptions. Here, she is more direct, as she talks
to her equal. The tone of voice, though still teacherly, is more confiding
here, these are comments about inferiors, people who don't see things as
they do. The diction of this aside is very different too, "disruptive
element in our midst" is not the language she would speak to the children
in. The contrast makes the simplicity of the surrounding lines more
apparent.
   The hustle and bustle of a primary school class is created by the short
sentences, which change in tone from endearment to frustration to almost
anger:

And don't punch Jacqueline.
I'm sure she didn't say she like you punching her, did you
Jacqueline?
Well I don't think it's a good idea so we won't have any more
punching.

"And" expresses some of the mounting irritation the speaker is trying
to suppress: it's yet another thing that's going wrong. By using
"Jacqueline", a feminine name for the victim, we assume, like the speaker,
that she is being "punched" against her will. Resorting to "I" rather than
"we" suggests how annoyed the speaker is at having her interpretation
rebuked. She resorts to using her authority to control them.
   Without describing them or allowing them even to speak, the writer
creates very specific pictures of the children. Susan, gregarious, enjoying
the attention she will get by offering her "lap"; Caroline, obedient,
pleased to help her teacher: Sidney, obviously intelligent, if a bit cheeky
– he sees that the teacher isn't quite right when she says "never" – yet

very likeable: David, wanting to show what he can do, and reluctant to give in - "No. Not today ... And not tomorrow"; Edgar and Neville, a no doubt notorious twosome.

In writing my parody, I have tried to mimic all these points. I found writing the short simple sentences, with no complicated words quite easy. Much more difficult was the mixture between formality, with the vocative commands:

Get down please.

and the informality of colloquial speech and sarcasm:

You'd rather go home? Bad luck.

The constant tension in the speaker's voice, which I hear almost verging on the shrill, and her sarcasm makes the piece funnier than just the children's misbehaviour could. The feeling that her ironic comments "because fishes don't like being held in people's hands" would be completely lost on the children adds to this humour. I found this aspect of the piece most difficult to mimic. Thinking of the problems the children could cause wasn't too difficult - I expect I did the same as the writer, and remembered what I'd seen or heard. Her writing certainly has the feel of being drawn directly from observation. It's also very funny!

Katherine Hodgson, a year twelve student

Sylvia Plath: "Daddy"

Describe the way Plath conveys the speaker's disturbed and contradictory feelings about her father in "Daddy". Look closely at particular images and the ways Plath exploits sounds, rhythms and changing tones of voice in her poem.

When this poem is read aloud, some parts in it seem to have the rhythm of a march, a terrifying march, as if an enormous army were approaching from the distance and you could hear thousands of feet stamping. These are the Nazi lines in "Daddy"; and not the words only but the sound and rhythm recreate the images of war in your mind: old flickering films, bombs falling, starved, tortured people, dead bodies... and the army itself - emotionless, machine-like, moving towards you under a glazed sky. And the wild, frightening music always accompanying these pictures. Someone told me about a child who was afraid of the German soldiers – those figures on the TV screen, not even knowing who or what they were. I remember that at the time when I didn't know anything about war or soldiers I was terrified of certain types of music. So it is in "Daddy" – the sound of them is just as important as the meaning of the words in evoking the feelings of wild terror.

The constantly repeating rhyme "oo" creates a mixed effect. Sometimes quite often there is a note of mockery in it and at the same time it is an accusation – like a pointed finger and a voice, maybe that of a small shrill child shouting out or a low full of hatred whispering : "You! You! You!" Or sometimes it is the sound of despair – like a groan or a suppressed cry. Sometimes a howl of pain. It is a sound of disgust or fear on which the entire poem is based.

The poem doesn't develop tension gradually: it starts with tension and then this tension grows till in the end it breaks like an over-tightened string on a violin. The first image of the girl's "daddy" is a black shoe:

> In which I have lived like a foot
> For thirty years, poor and white
> Barely daring to breathe or Achoo

This may or may not have a connection with the nursery rhyme about an old woman who lived in a shoe, a rhyme which a child would be expected to find simply funny but which is, if you get rid of the childish associations, a much more complicated and sad idea. In "Daddy" it describes a psychological condition which a claustrophobic trapped in a small room could experience. She feels her Daddy has been smothering, pinching, confining her against her will.

And the speaker calls him:

> marble heavy, a bag full of God

He died when she was only ten and became a burden she had to lug through life. She was too young ever to have fully known or understood him and his death raised him above all other people and in his daughter's eyes he could never have any faults. He became an "idol", a marble monument. "Mummy" never appears in the poem; the speaker appears to have a relationship only with her (dead and imaginary) "Daddy". Perhaps her mother could/would not discuss HIM: he was a mystery like God. People believe that God exists but they do not know what he looks like, why he behaves as he does, what he is thinking: and the daughter feared and worshipped the father – not the one who lived but the idealised figure conjured up by her imagination, needs and fears. In fact all she remembers of him are snippets like:

> a head in the freakish Atlantic
> Where it pours bean green over blue
> In waters of beautiful Nauset

It is the one unspoilt, lovely and lyrical moment in the poem, her one happy memory and it seems to be associated with a real man who lived (and swam) in this world. His daughter still calls him "daddy" as she called him then. The "daddy" who lives in her mind now, who has been haunting and terrifying her for years, is not that "daddy" of her childhood.

That happy, peaceful memory of her father is squeezed out of her by images of Germans from wartime posters and films: all sorts of propaganda and half-truths. Her weak, uncritical childish love of her German father was sabotaged by everyone's hatred of Germans. Every German now seemed to be a fascist, and all Germans were him. Germany, Germans, the German language became associated only with destruction, brutality and torture.

The girl's father originated from a Polish town

> Scraped flat by the roller
> Of wars, wars, wars

His language which she could never master was like a "barb wire snare" in which her sensitive tongue was savagely trapped. And even more frightening the harsh guttural sounds suggest the sounds of a concentration camp transport train "chuffing" victims off to Dachau, Aushwitz and Belsen.

The daughter now identifies herself with the Nazi victims, the Jews: she wants to be a Jew, she feels like a Jew: battered psychologically by a "Daddy" as the victims were tortured in the camps by a black impersonal hatred symbolised by everything that is the opposite of God: a black swastika: the crooked cross.

Her imaginary father's figure swells out to be a symbol of evil when she mentions his "neat moustache" and "aryan eye" and calls him "panzer man": he becomes Hitler himself: the devil incarnate. The word "you" suddenly appears with a capital "Y": she even calls him a "devil". Her love and worshipping of her god-like father dissolves into a hatred of a Fascist. Instead of the blue and green of her childhood memories: black now appears in the only photograph she has of him: black man at a black board: the black man who

> bit my pretty red heart in two

"Daddy" collage by Polina Bakhnova, a year twelve student.

The meaning of the word "Daddy" and the tone in which she articulates it has changed completely. He is not even a "ghastly statue with one grey toe": he is

> Not God but a swastika
> So black no sky could squeak through

What also makes this figure frightening is irony. The daughter laughs at him, remembering how she was trying to kill herself in a desperate attempt to be reunited with the daddy she was passionately yearned for:

> But they pulled me out of the sack
> And they stuck me together with glue

at women:

> Every woman adores a Fascist
> The boot in the face, the brute
> Brute heart of a brute like you

or rather what men pretend to themselves a woman "adores". The speaker's hatred of her father is developing into hatred of the whole sex. It is not a quiet humorous irony of Jewish people laughing at their "weird luck" it is an almost hysterical laughter, mockery that conveys a terrifyingly pure hatred.

When the words and expressions are repeated, it does not only draw attention to the words but makes them sound like chanting. As in the middle and nearer to the end of the poem tension grows and lines seem to be said all in one breath, it looks as if the speaker's hatred of Fascism has gained a strength equal to the strength of Fascism itself: after all, Hitler was finally incinerated himself. To me, the daughter's hatred seems just as frightening as the image of her fantasy father and this hatred is destroying her from within: she now despises herself for being his adoring daughter, trying to be good enough for him, for marrying a man who resembled him and by this trying to recover him:

> And then I knew what to do
> I made a model of you
> A man in black with a Meinkampf look

> And a love of the rack and the screw
> And I said "I do. I do..."

The rack and the screw are instruments of torture. Her marriage was seven years of being a victim. Through a clever switch of imagery she now stumbles upon a way to find relief. Her husband was like a vampire who

drank my blood.

But as all know from the movies, vampires, like husbands, can be disposed of. (I doubt she literally "killed" her husband but freeing herself from him she showed she could free herself from "Daddy" too if she wanted to.)

It is at this stage of her life, after living seven years with

the vampire who said he was you

she suddenly realises that it was not her father at all that she hated. It is not him she calls a "bastard" at the end of the poem but a phoney (bastard) father: the figure her imagination had created and who had tortured her all her life. She doesn't need to kill him but that enormous, unreal figure, the marble monument full of God-Devil that lay heavy on her shoulders, trapping her from developing an individual self. All that castle of hatred and resentment she built around herself has no foundation – and it crashes.

I don't think any relationship between father and daughter was possible after that. She could only destroy all her memories of him, assure herself that he never existed (any more than vampires exist) and start her life anew: free.

Polina Bakhnova, a year twelve student

Charles Dickens: *Hard Times*

What impression of the town and its inhabitants does Dickens give you in this extract? Write an essay quoting the details which help to give you those impressions and examine the way Dickens's diction, imagery, rhythm and sentence-structure convey them to you.

interminable serpents of smoke trailed themselves for ever and ever and never got uncoiled

This is a typical example of the impression given by Dickens of the town: an industrialised town where smog fills the air and coats the buildings

brick that would have been red if the smoke and ashes had allowed it

Where the river is polluted with "ill-smelling dyes", the buildings "rattling and trembling" from the incessant machinery and the sun itself unable to penetrate the "heavy vapour drooping over Coketown".

Coketown is a melancholy place from the "factory yards" and "frying oil" and is not popular with the author, who conveys his intense dislike of the place. He condemns the dirty, dusty appearance of the town i) by likening the buildings to "the painted face of a savage" and ii) by saying it represents death more than life "engendering more death than life".

These comparisons are extremely negative, they represent evil. They convey that the town is a bad place where only evil lurks. This idea of death and evil is created by words such as "savage" and the idea that the good sunlight cannot get through the cloudy atmosphere.

Cara de le Mare, a year twelve student

* * * * *

I think the most important word in this passage is for Dickens "unnatural". The whole place is presented to us as a man-made hell-on-earth where everything God-given, healthy and good: sunlight, water, air: has been spoiled and turned into something terrifying, dangerous and ultimately life-destroying. The "interminable serpents of smoke" have triumphed and Paradise is only a distant memory.

The people have lost their humanity and become like cogs in a never stopping machine: the town is its industry, just one big machine, and human needs are ignored, all that matters is production. "People" are just the jobs they do : "stokers" or whatever : merely a factor of production. We get the feeling that there are no human bosses : the workers are at the beck and call of some superhuman, impersonal force which controls their lives and owns their bodies. Dickens is showing the foul face of Capitalism.

Coketown's name says it all: it is a place producing Coke, run on Coke, smelling of Coke: life is work and the town has no other side to it. These people are not working to live but living to work. Their lives are a relentless routine in foul, oppressive conditions. Things are so bad that when the sun comes instead of bringing relief it actually makes things worse. The greenhouse effect.

The inhabitants have no names, no identities anymore, they have become numbers. Dickens uses lots of repetition in the passage to emphasise the dreadful monotony of the people's existences : they are worn down by it all into anonymity:

like one another....like one another....like one another

mimics the clockwork routine of the workers and mimics the relentless rhythm of the machines which never stop or even vary their pace.

same... same... same.... same....

like a conveyer belt. Work has no sense of pride for the workers, they are just standing in for the machines which will ultimately be invented to make them totally unnecessary. People don't matter, just profit.

Dickens is a sentimental writer and uses lots of pathos here to make his political points. The kids in the "crazy" boat are interesting. We can't stop ourselves feeling very protective to them as they risk tumbling into "the river that was black and thick with dye" and giving off "vile smells". We feel helpless and angry. The whole environment is life-destroying which, Dickens seems to be implying is what the Industrial Revolution is: "engendering more death than life".

Chris Verity, a year thirteen student

* * * * *

A town all built of red brick is bad enough but this has become worse than monotonous, it is frightening and aggressive "like a savage".

Everything in the town has been polluted by the "interminable serpents of smoke" and poisonous waste discharged. The word "interminable" conveys what it means by the way you say it: will the word ever end? The long vowel sound on "ter" is tedious. And we think of the image of the serpent in the Garden of Eden: everything lovely and natural is being corrupted, poisoned.

It is quite a surreal and hostile world with its "river that ran purple with ill-smelling dyes" assaulting your eyes and nose and the terrible, never-ending noise and vibration of the machines: "a rattling and a trembling all day long".

You feel battered by it all and no wonder the people seem like robots who have been desensitised by their ugly environment. What sort of people could thrive in such an ugly, hostile place? They are like robots now, with few human characteristics left because such things as individualism and imagination are not wanted in a factory-town, just obedience and slavery.

Dickens emphasises routine and conformity :

..several large streets all very like one another, and many small
streets still more like one another, inhabited by people equally
like one another.....

This is so odd coming from Dickens who usually introduces everyone in a
novel as an individual eccentric, quite unlike anyone else. These people
have ceased to have personalities. The rhythm of this whole section is
pounding like the machines: the natural rhythms of life have been replaced
by the rhythms of the piston-rods.

I find the image of "the head of an elephant in a state of melancholy
madness" very disturbing. Elephants are large, clumsy but usually rather
friendly creatures but these ones (really the pistons of steam engines) like
the people are not as nature intended but "melancholy mad": the word "melancholy" has a heavy, sad tone to it as well as sounding as if it will go on
for ever.

The poor stokers emerge from their "low underground doorways" like
prisoners being allowed a little fresh air only to be tortured by the
sunlight which like everything else in Coketown has been perverted from
being good to being harmful (like the depletion of the ozone layer has made
sunshine for us a hazard). The idea of humans "frying in oil" is very upset-
ting; there is no fresh air: we panic with claustrophobia. I don't understand what the "fairy palaces" are but Dickens must be being sarcastic here,
there is no magic in Coketown. The imagery of desert heat and dryness is
uncomfortable. We long for water. Then when at the end we finally get water,
there is no relief because the water the boys are playing on is like poison:
"black and thick with dye".

It is like a nightmare from which you can't wake up.

James Baldwin, a year thirteen student

George Eliot: *Middlemarch*

*a) What impression of Edward Casaubon do you think George Eliot intends to
convey to the reader of the novel? With close attention to particular details,
examine the means by which she does it.*

I think George Eliot intends the reader to find Casaubon as a very
bizarre character to be a suitor, or writing a letter of proposal. His letter

is certainly not the sort of thing one would expect in a proposal. The idea
of marriage is not mentioned until the end of the second paragraph: where it
is called a "matrimonial union".

This phrase would be more at home in a letter written by a lawyer or
business man. This type of diction is used throughout the letter. The word
"love" doesn't appear once but we are told that the letter is an "accurate
statement of [his] feelings", a phrase which seems to contain very little if
any emotion or feeling! The expression would be more appropriate for a list
of his possessions; he has nothing more and nothing less in the way of
"feeling" for her.

The diction and the syntax used in the letter make the thought of a
woman accepting this proposal seem ludicrous:

> I am not, I trust, mistaken in the recognition of some deeper
> correspondence ...... consciousness of need ...... arisen
> contemporaneously ....

This one sentence is so wordy and long, it becomes tedious to read. The
polysyllabic words and contorted structure used make it clumsy and cumber-
some to read, but the letter has probably been well thought-out and planned,
as the writer comes across to be a highly educated man of a high standing.
He believes in doing what is proper and correct in his society as he has her
guardian's "permission to address" Miss Brooke so he would not think of
sending a letter that had not been correctly thought out.

However the letter conveys no feelings of passion, which one would
normally associate with a proposal.

The rhythm of the letter is very steady, it has no vitality, life or
energy. Perhaps Eliot is using this as a direct reflection of Mr Casaubon.
Eliot is conveying to the reader that this character is not a young man with
lots of energy: "Of life .... short in the sequel".

He is an old man which may explain the dull and tedious tone of the
letter. However Eliot tells us that the other character, Miss Brooke, the
girl to whom the proposal is written is quite young: in the "early bloom of
youth". For me this raises the question of how she could want to marry this
stuffy old man and why he wants her.

As I said earlier this letter would be better coming from a businessman
and perhaps this proposed marriage is more like a partnership. Mr Casaubon
has discovered a "need in [his] own life" and has decided that this girl is
in possession of "perhaps exclusive fitness to supply that need". This character is obviously not experienced in flattery (as he later admits: "in
this order of experience I am still young,") as the word "perhaps" doesn't

endear me to him. The notion of doubt should not exist in a proposal, she should be the only one.

The point that she can "supply" his "need" makes her sound like a secretary or a hatstand. This is a marriage (or will be) of convenience, Mr Casaubon's convenience, as Eliot indicates with Mr Casaubon using a high frequency of personal pronouns. Thus giving the reader the impression that this character is very self-important and opinionated. The complex words and syntax Eliot gives him that contain very little substance show the grand impressions he wants (or Eliot wants him) to convey: "contemporaneously", "dissimulate", "superficially".

He flatters Miss Brooke by complimenting her intellect: "in you an elevation of thought".

She certainly needs it to be able to understand this marriage proposal! Eliot gives us the impression that this character thinks he is bestowing great honour on this girl by giving her the privilege of marrying him: "I can at least offer you an affection hitherto unwasted," and to fit into his life: "clear to you the tenor of my life and purposes;" which no uneducated person could: "unsuited, ... to the commoner order of minds".

The more the reader reads this letter the more you begin to feel sorry for Miss Brooke who has been an object for Mr Casaubon's "observation" and now is worthy of helping the "consecration of a life."

Eliot makes the reader laugh in desperation at this letter as it is so inflated and awkward for a proposal. I just hope that either Miss Brooke declines the offer eloquently or that Mr Casaubon will die in the near future and let the poor girl have a life of her own not of the "earthly guardian of your welfare," who sounds as far from a lover or fiancé as you can get.

Lisa Chotia, a year twelve student

b) *Imagine yourself as Miss Brooke. Write a reply to Mr Casaubon's letter in what you think would be an appropriate style. Then write a commentary on what you have written, explaining how particular aspects of the style of the original letter have influenced the style of your own.*

Mr Casaubon,

I can honestly inform you that I was in no way intent on having erroneously elevated your hopes however "temporarily". For, despite the reciprocal nature of the appreciation of each other's intelligence, there is very little I feel you could return to me, in the way of genuine affection (apart from the self-appreciative form of a grateful master, who is able to congratulate himself fully as to the aptness of his choice of servant with whom it is as pleasing to regard as to converse) that could in anyway satisfy my needs. I would, however like to take this opportunity in order that I might prevent any like embarrassments from reoccuring.

I am greatly flattered by the compliments you have paid to my uncommon intelligence and gravity, but feel that I am bound to impart to you the idea that I might be capable of some great work of my own origin without it being necessary for me to merely assist you in yours, however important it be. Despite your feeling that beauty and elevation of mind may have been mutually exclusive, I would like you to consider that it is both presumptuous and insulting to assume that in my person you can fill two gaps in your life, simultaneously finding a pretty young wife, and a supremely competent secretary. Should it be that your life's plan requires that you are blessed with a reprieve of your solitariness and your work burden (as, I feel compelled to add, will be to a certain degree necessary as old age encroaches, for, despite my feeling relative to myself, I am certainly appreciative of the gravity and significance of your work) I would suggest you look for two people, each to fill an independent void, as no woman who has both the beauty and tenor of mind you have attributed to me would ever feel complete being but your housekeeper and secretary, without being more convinced of the sincerity of your affection.

I hope that you find this letter neither too hurtful nor embarrassing, and that we may continue to be friends.

Dorothea Brooke.

The greatest temptation in writing Dorothea's reply was to make it short and curt. However, both the clues given as to her character through the response she provoked in Casaubon, and the way in which his letter was written made me opt for a style that attempted to echo his.

As the recipient of his letter, I would be overwhelmed. He is convinced of the clarity of his question, his "accurate statement of (his) feelings" yet the complex and exceptionally long sentences, coupled with the formal language "contemporaneously", "superficially coincident with foreshadowing needs, but providentially related thereto ..." makes this letter very hard to understand. It is possible to assume that this is a man "still young", in this "order of experience" if not in life in general, yet in his inability to express emotion – he never speaks of love, only "affection" and a "matrimonial union" – and is made more remote by his legal-sounding language:

impression of your eminent and perhaps exclusive fitness to supply
that need ... with the mental qualities above indicated.

This "union" is described more like a formal reverse of a job applica-
tion. Dorothea is suitable because she will "supply that need", because she
is seen as unusual, but not, I feel, unique, in having the "fitness" for
this position.

To an objective reader, it is quite clear how comic Casaubon's letter
is, how condescending the tone, how inflated the language. In replying to it
as Dorothea, I had to imagine myself the recipient of a serious letter, one
sent with my "guardian's permission". Casaubon may be presented as a fool,
but he is intelligent to some degree, and I feel I could trust that he was
not "mistaken" as to the "recognition of some deeper correspondence". I had
to consider myself a beautiful young woman, with both an "elevation of
thought and a capability of devotedness".

More difficult was to imagine how I would have felt in 1871 or earlier,
before feminism and the emancipation of women. In writing my reply I assumed
the qualities Casaubon gave me were true, and that as well as "tenor", I had
strength of conviction. The essence of the reply, an explained rejection,
was my own reaction to this emotionless love letter. I chose to write in a
style which directly emulated Casaubon's own because I felt this was the
language he would best understand. Although the letter reads like at least a
sixth draft, I do feel this is the way in which Casaubon thinks. I copied
his habit of interrupting himself with brackets:

(connected, I may say ....)
(which, let me say again..)

This creates the impression of exactness whilst confusing the reader
further by causing them to lose their train of thought. I would have liked
to use as many first person pronouns as Casaubon does, as this creates a
very strong impression of being self-centred and selfish. I didn't find this
easy as the description of Dorothea as having a "capability of devotedness"
suggested to me that she was the one who cared, and who would try to be
constructive in her criticism.

The opening and close of the letter gave a strong impression.

My Dear Miss Brooke,
               ....
Edward Casaubon.

Dorothea is already his, and throughout the letter she is treated as a commodity, a business proposition. Whilst not liking to judge a man by his name, "Edward Casaubon" was chosen by George Eliot in order to create a specific impression of justness and reserve. To address Mr Casaubon I dropped the "My Dear" as being both inappropriate to a rejection and to the impression I obtained of Dorothea. In my reply, I am aware that there are too many twentieth century thoughts and assumptions for it to read as a genuine reply. It is however, how I would respond if I were in such a situation and had such attitudes as Casaubon indicates.

Katherine Hodgson, a year twelve student

Toni Morrison: *The Bluest Eye*

Write an essay examining the impact on you of the opening of Toni Morrison's novel, **The Bluest Eye.** *Describe what you feel the writer was trying to achieve by structuring the beginning of her novel and the kind of novel this opening leads you to expect.*

The structure of the opening of the novel consists of three separate but repeated paragraphs followed by a section in italicised type. The content of the first three paragraphs is quite a surprise as the language used is simple, childlike language. The content of these paragraphs is identical but each is set out differently.

The first paragraphs are in prose, however not the prose that you would expect to see in an adult piece of literature like this one. It is written in child's reading-book basic language, in short disjointed sentences. The first paragraph seems pleasant, talking of happy family life with an ideal family. But as it is repeated it starts to become threatening and disturbing like a repetitive nightmare. The words remain the same and the same size but the lines become closer together, and the words get smaller spaces in between and punctuation is missed out which adds to the claustrophobic effect.

It is difficult to make a judgement about the whole novel by looking at the opening five paragraphs. However the first three suggest that a happy family life is not the theme. It is as though this portrayal of a so-called perfect life is being drummed into someone, maybe being used as a contrast to someone's not-so-happy lifestyle. It talks of the house being "very pretty" and the family being "very happy". Drumming it in like this suggests the book being about troubles in the family. This impression is supported by the italicised paragraphs. After the emphasis being put on happy families, what follows raises the issue of incest in only the second line.

At this stage it is difficult to know whether the people in the first paragraphs: "Mother, father, Jane and Dick" are connected with the characters in the italicised paragraphs, or whether these are just reading-book characters presented just as a contrast to the very different families of real life.

You can immediately see that all is not well in the second part of the opening chapter when Morrison talks of Pecola having "her father's baby".

The idea of marigolds not sprouting in the fall of 1941 is talked about more than Pecola and her father's baby not surviving. Marigolds is the first things said and then the issue with Pecola is mentioned afterwards every time. This gives the feeling that something is trying to be blanked out by the person talking; maybe it is too painful to remember: "But so deeply concerned were we with the health and safe delivery of Pecola's baby we could think nothing but our own magic".

However, when Morrison writes "we had dropped our seeds in our own little plot of black dirt just as Pecola's father had dropped his seeds in his own plot of black dirt" there is a distinct sound of contempt towards Pecola's father in the speaker's voice. She effectively contrasts the innocence of two children planting seeds in their garden with the issue of incest between the father and Pecola, by the use of metaphorical language.

The paragraph ends by reminiscing, but not about pleasant times:

Cholly Breedlove is dead; our innocence too. The seeds
shrivelled and died; her baby too.

It ends with the speaker wanting to know why or how it happened – needing to know the reason for the incidents of the fall of 1941.

When you read the "happy" opening after reading through the whole chapter, you begin to find some sinister things present even in what seemed to be a pretty and safe setting. I now find the last sentences very scary:

Run, dog, run. Look, look. Here comes a friend. The friend will
play with Jane. They will play a good game. Play, Jane, play.

After reading about what happened to Pecola, I think the game this mysterious "friend" will play may be anything but a "good game". It's creepy the way the dog runs off as the "friend" approaches.

Alison Scott, a year twelve student

Thom Gunn: "Human Condition"

With close attention to the ways the ideas are presented, examine the picture of the "Human Condition" Thom Gunn paints in his poem.

What struck me first about this poem was its tight structure: six stanzas of six lines each, every line with six syllables: 216 syllables in all! As if the poet was trying to get all his ideas expressed as economically and strictly as possible. There is a totally regular and tricky rhyme structure too: abcbca: though some of the rhymes are only half-rhymes: "visible/individual" in stanza two for example and "universe/own use" in stanza four. (I've just realised that some lines have extra syllables too: lines one and six of stanza three and lines two and four of stanza four.)

But these exceptions don't alter the impression that the whole poem has been very carefully put together, very deliberately shaped. The rhythm is a regular three stresses to a line : de-dum de-dum de- dum: except for the lines already mentioned where there is an extra unstressed syllable (a bit untidily) at the end of the line:

> In the established border...
> The neighbouring disorder.

Given that the rest of the poem is so highly disciplined, I think this is probably a deliberate effect: suggesting that the "border" is difficult to keep to, there's always the risk of "disorder".

However, although the structure of the poem can be analysed like this and shown to be very strict, when you read the poem the first few times you're not fully aware of the control the poet has. You hear some rhymes such as "coat" and "moat" straight away because they are stressed at the ends of lines. But because the punctuation in the poem is so flexible, the ends of lines (and hence the rhyming words) are not always emphasised so much and the rhythm is close to the rhythm of natural speech.

In the first stanza, for example, the first pause comes not at the end of the first line but half-way, the sentence then running on to be completed by the second line:

> Now it is fog, I walk
> Contained within my coat;

In stanza three this process goes even further: neither of the first two lines is end-stopped and the sentence reads very much like prose:

> In the established border
> There balances a mere
> Pinpoint of consciousness;

The other thing which makes the poem so unlike a lyrical poem (even though it is shaped like one) is the diction which is very ordinary, prosaic. There's nothing song-like about words such as "Contained"..."mercenaries'"... "condemned"... "consciousness" or "disordered", for example. It's much more the language of an essay or a speech than what you expect to find in a song.

This is anticipated by the title of the poem "Human Condition" which you might expect to see as the title of a book in the Philosophy section of a library. It leads you to expect a heavyweight investigation into "What It Means to be Human" or a serious-toned study of "The State of Mankind in the Twentieth Century".

In a way, that is what the poem tries to do: like some other of Thom Gunn's poems which I've read such as "On the Move" this is a bit of philosophy-in-verse, the poet deliberately trying to fit serious and searching ideas into a tight package: seeing if he can say something significant about the "Human Condition" in just a hundred and fifty words or so.

There's something very dry about the language: no passion or humour like you get when Lawrence tackles "philosophical" ideas in his poems: it's all a bit too cool and collected for my taste. You feel the poet has sorted everything out in his own mind and is now passing it on to us. You don't get the sense that the speaker is anyone but the poet himself (as you do when you read something like Eliot's "Prufrock"). We are expected to take what is said here seriously and at face value.

As in "On the Move" the poem explores the idea that we are all basically on our own:

> I stay or start from here:
> I am my one touchstone.

There are no signposts or friends to help you on your way through life (the street lamps are feeble) : being human means being utterly alone:

> No castle more cut off
> By reason of its moat...

But although this begins as a gloomy idea, literally a life-sentence:

> I am condemned to be an individual

By the end of the poem, the speaker's tone has become more enthusiastic:

I...
Walk through hypothesis,
An individual."

Fog has become nothing to worry about; just trust your instincts.

Jo Ramsey, a year thirteen student

* * * * *

A poem with a very ambitious title: La Condition Humaine.
The poem begins with the dramatic idea:

Now it is fog...

It hasn't always been like this. Once I/we/mankind could see where it was and where it was heading but

Now it is fog...

Like the fog that billows around everyone at the beginning of Dickens's "Bleak House" or in Eliot's "Prufrock", this is clearly metaphorical fog: mental confusion, muddle, a sense of being cut-off, isolated from others:

No castle more cut off...

There are other people around but they don't sound friendly:

...the sentry's cough,
The mercenaries' talk.

Mercenaries kill for cash; the sentry sounds nervous...
Rather oddly Gunn switches from this medieval setting to a very modern one:

The street-lamps...
Drop no light...
But press beams painfully

The lamps sound almost human, trying hard to penetrate the fog but failing pathetically. Everywhere there is fog:

    ... a yard of fog around

That "yard" may be a measure or it may be the whole world is our "yard", our dwelling place. Whichever is the case, the streetlamps aren't going to be much help. We're isolated, cut off, alone and feeling threatened by whatever may be lurking in the fog...

I'm not at all sure what "border" the poet is talking about in the third stanza. He says it's "established" : does that mean "taken for granted" or "negotiated"? It seems to be where we are in our human voyage: "I stay or start from here..."

Two stanzas later he says "I am my one touchstone." and I think this means that all any of us has got is ourselves, our "Pinpoint of conscious-ness".

"We think therefore we exist" but we can't be certain of anything else. The poem has this sceptical feel about it:

    Particular, I must
    Find out...

"Particular" is a pun here (Plath uses the same pun in "Spinster"): the speaker describes himself as a particular person:

    An individual

who's very "particular" to see things as clearly as possible (at least in his head: outside there is only fog). You feel the speaker is trying to hammer it all out, get things straight in his mind: "To pick thought and sensation..."

"pick" here meaning both "pick my way" and "choose". The poem is very much about choosing to take control of your destiny. When the idea comes first that we are all alone in the universe it sounds very threatening:

    I am condemned to be
    An individual.

Cut off, alone, vulnerable, weak.... "condemned" by God? Fate? We're not sure who's in control.

But as the poem develops, the speaker seems to take up the challenge:

I seek, to break my span.

This sounds like a reference to the Renaissance idea of "man as the measure of all things" but taken a stage further. By finding out your limits (span) you can then try to go beyond them. Of course we cannot go beyond our lifespan... or can we? Suddenly there is a note of heroic defiance in the poem. Instead of feeling sorry that he's human, the speaker now seems to want to hang on to that:

I keep my guard
On that which makes me man.

The poem is very much a product of the twentieth century : an expression of defiance born out of despair. In the past, perhaps, there were "certainties", things that could be trusted, like God or the family or the State. With so much knowledge we can feel simply confused, overwhelmed, lost in the fog. But alternatively we can turn things round as the speaker does here and accept that:

Much is unknowable...

Worry and self-doubt can become an excuse for self-pity and laziness (as with Eliot's Prufrock). This speaker seems to have decided that you shouldn't waste time facing problems until they arise. Although we're born into a foggy wasteland we can stride forward with confidence rejoicing in the fact that we alone choose our destinies:

Walk through hypothesis
An individual.

The ending has a tone of confidence and determination about it, as if the fog has become so many cobwebs to be brushed aside.

Nick Adams, a mature, Access student

Henry James: *What Maisie Knew*

Write an essay in which you explore what you take to be the purpose of the Preamble to James's novel **What Maisie Knew**. *Describe some of the techniques James uses to achieve the effects he does.*

James's preamble to "What Maisie Knew" serves several purposes. Most importantly it establishes his tone of ironic detachment. It also allows him to introduce the principal characters. He presents them in a dispassionate and perfectly balanced manner, yet leaves the reader with little doubt as to how vile Ida and Beale really are!

A natural distance is formed between the reader and Maisie. James achieves this by presenting Maisie not directly, but through references from other characters. However, it is virtually impossible to read these first four pages without experiencing feelings of anger, disgust, frustration and sympathy, aroused due to our natural instinct to protect the child.

At times James does appeal to the heart, rather than the intellect, but he narrowly avoids making Maisie a sentimental character, despite liberal use of words such as "innocence", "child", and more alarmingly, the dangerously Dickensian "little".

The novel opens with an account of Ida and Beale's divorce. Their competitive spirit is instantly made obvious as they treat the divorce like a game. Maisie is conspicuous only by her absence. Her role in the proceedings is passive, her future is simply referred to as "the assignment of the child". She has no influence, as the focus is centred around Ida and Beale. This heightens the reader's concern as it is clear that there is no interest in Maisie as a child, but only as a pawn in their "fierce pursuance of this triumph".

They want to gain custody of Maisie not for love, but for victory. Maisie is yet again dehumanised - reduced to the level of a prize, or more appropriately, a weapon to aid their attack. It was Beale who "won" Maisie, but not because he was more suitable, or responsible. As James observes, by the end of the trial he was "bespattered from head to foot" as a result of Ida's accusations. He "won" because he was a man! An immoral woman was considered to be far worse than an immoral man: "the brilliance of a lady's complexion might be more regarded as showing the spots".

James meticulously balances their faults - they are shown to be as bad as each other. To maintain this balance, he cannot allow Beale to have triumphed completely, so enforces a "condition" on the custody. The court orders that Beale should refund to Ida "the twenty-six hundred pounds put down by her" for Maisie's up-keep. It establishes our sense of Beale's irresponsibility as he has clearly spent the money and has no means of paying it back! ("...a sum of which he had had the administration and of which he could render the least account...")

The balance is now restored. For Ida it "...drew a part of the sting from her defeat". Beale was compelled to "...perceptively lower his crest". Appropriate imagery. Beale is very showy, and "crest" makes me imagine a bird's splendid plumage. In contrast to this Beale's finery is very artificial. It is a perfect balance James strives to maintain. Occasionally it feels too contrived – more convenient than credible?

Their childish and aggressive attitude to their divorce is exemplified when James comments "that after a squabble scarcely less public and scarcely more decent...", having described the divorce as a "battle", they eventually reached a "compromise" concerning the settlement. Typically this "compromise" is ironic – it is in neither Beale nor Ida's nature to compromise, both work in extremes. Both are selfish and stubborn. If they were genuinely concerned about money, they wouldn't pay for the expense of going through a court. I think that their enjoyment of battle, and public attention, was of more importance to them than the money.

We learn of the dreadful agreement concerning how Maisie is to be "disposed" of: "She was divided in two and the portions tossed impartially to the disputants..." James compares this terrible arrangement to "...the judgement seat of Solomon". An ironic comparison because the careless attitude of the Faranges is completely opposed to the compassionate attitude of the real mother in Solomon, who gives up her child to the imposter, rather than see it harmed. In contrast, the Faranges don't even consider the effect this potentially disastrous arrangement will have on Maisie's development.

Maisie is to spend six months with each parent, and "...neither parent figured as a happy example to youth and innocence." As both Ida and Beale are clearly unsuitable to be parents, a "proper third person" was searched for. It soon became apparent that amongst the Faranges "circle" there was no such "proper" person, so the search was lowered to "...some respectable or at least presentable friend". "Presentable" suggests that appearance is again of more importance than substance. James stresses that superficiality when he comments that "...the circle of the Faranges had been scanned in vain for any such ornament...". The Faranges life revolves around such "ornaments": shallow friends, fine clothes and, of course, money. There is no room for a child. I cannot help but wonder if Maisie was a "mistake".

Both parents realised that Maisie would be a useful tool to amplify their social status. They felt that "... after being perfectly insignificant together they would be decidedly striking apart". Again, the emphasis is on appearance and superficial social status – people were interested in them because they provided exciting gossip! They had "...produced an impression that warranted people in looking for appeals in the newspaper for the rescue of the the little one", which was dramatic enough for the "vociferous public". People loved speculating about Maisie's fate, but only one person surpassed mock concern and actually did something. She proposed taking over Ida's "shift". This would be quite unremarkable had it not led to a revealing section of dialogue capturing Ida's attitude perfectly. She refers to Beale as "that low brute", and is not afraid to state that she "detests him most". The woman, one of few people who has Maisie's interests at heart, sensibly points out that if Ida wishes Maisie to forget Beale, it will be impossible whilst she keeps "... him before her by perpetually abusing him". This is true of both parents – neither is interested in Maisie for her value as a human being, but only to exploit her, making her attack and hurt the other parent. Ida and Beale are obsessive and passionate in their hatred for each other. Ironically, I suspect that these feelings of hate are stronger than any feelings of love they once had for one another.

Neither considers how hurtful and confusing it would be for Maisie constantly having to listen to her "other" parent being abused. "The good lady's (who offered to care for Maisie) silence was a "grim judgement" ... the silence was broken as she exclaimed "Poor little monkey!" These words were described by James as "...as epitaph for the tomb of Maisie's child-hood" at the age of five or six. How can her childhood die before it has properly begun? The image of a tomb is frightening as it's obviously associ-ated with death. We pity Maisie's vulnerability as "... she was abandoned to her fate". The word "abandoned" stresses the injustice of the situation, and emphasises Maisie's helplessness. The reader finds Maisie's predicament terrible, but at the same time it appeals to our protective instincts.

James leaves us in no doubt that Ida and Beale do not love Maisie, as he says: "What was clear to any spectator was that the only link binding her to any parent was this lamentable fact of her being a ready vessel for bitterness..." Again the imagery is hurtful, as Maisie is represented as the pure white, porcelain cup (therefore innocent, fragile, vulnerable and deli-cate). "... a deep little porcelain cup in which biting acids could be mixed". The reader knows how harmful acid is, but as James emphasises the damage by saying "biting acids" it becomes even more painful.

Maisie is trapped, unable to defend herself unconsciously other than with the "protective layer" of her innocence. Her parents wanted her ".. for the harm they could, with her unconscious aid, do each other". the fact that it is her "unconscious aid" angers me. They are manipulating her for their evil intentions and it will harm her when she understands, and of course she will understand far too soon.

James works hards to reinforce the equality between Ida and Beale. Both want revenge, both have been "... alike crippled by the heavy hand of justice". An ironic comment; it is hardly "justice" for Maisie, who should be the most important person considered in the "judgement", but it is hardly considered at all. I think that they deserve the "heavy hand of justice" as they brought it upon themselves through their enthusiastically vicious attacks in court. Both were trying to "get everything". They were "... both as bad, indeed, since they were only so good as each other". Ida wanted to prevent Beale from "so much as looking" at Maisie, and Beale thought that Ida's "... slightest touch was simply contamination". Maisie had to combine the two parents' hatred of each other, and to try to make some sense of her situation.

James offers us reassurance amongst this pessimism as he comments directly to the reader:

> There were persons horrified to think what those in charge of it would combine to try to make of it: no one could conceive in advance that they would be able to make nothing ill.

Although this preliminary chapter is written as if an outsider is giving an unbiased account of the divorce, rather than the situation as it is seen through Maisie's eyes it is unusual for James to give us such a direct insight into Maisie's future. James's great faith in Maisie's "little unspotted soul" over-powers most doubts the reader has about the feasibility of Maisie's continued innocence. In theory we feel that Maisie would be affected by her corrupt surroundings and companions, and as a result of this would become a brat!

Georgina Leeson, a year thirteen student

* * * * *

The novel "What Maisie Knew" begins with a short opening chapter which serves the same purpose as a prologue in a play – it introduces us to the characters and events preceding the action which we are about to see and gives us a certain idea of what this action might be about. The four pages are indeed packed with information: the brief description of the legal case, its result, its effect, the society and its preoccupation with the scandal and the introduction to Ida and Beale.

The description of Ida and Beale Farange at the end of the opening chapter sums up their characters. Somehow we instinctively feel that this is the beginning and the end of their personalities and that we should not expect a deep psychological investigation. What convinces us is the Dickensian quality of this description: quick flashes of their attitudes towards each other and the situation related in a few words and clearly ironical way, images, the most noticeable feature of their appearance underlined, extended to the size of caricature and become their characteristics like Beale's teeth and Ida's long arms – "the length being conducive perhaps to not having so often beaten her ex-husband at billiards, a game in which she showed superiority largely accountable, as she maintained, for the resentment finding expression in his physical violence".

But then, James is not concerned with the psychological investigation – the only person in whose mind we'll be able to peer is Maisie. James asks questions rather than gives answers; it is up to us to make judgements – all this doesn't make "What Maisie Knew" a psychological novel – and the opening chapter is not an introduction to such. It is more an introduction to action which is to follow. The play is cast, the roles are taken up and presented to us, the chess-pieces are all put in the right places and the game will now begin.

It is a chess game in which Maisie is caught and used as a pawn, at least this is how James presents it to us in the opening chapter – there is a symmetry between the two parents, neither is better than the other – we have two identical parties at war with each other. They are identical in their style and their effect on people in their society. "Like her husband she (Ida) carried clothes, carried them as a train carries passengers: people had been know to compare their taste and dispute about the accommodation they gave these articles, though inclining on the whole to the conversation of Ida as less overcrowded, especially with jewellery and flowers...They made up together, for instance, some twelve feet three of stature, and nothing was more discussed than the apportionment of this quantity". They are described and viewed here by society as two matching pieces of decorative furniture, yet when they are separated and no longer necessarily associated with each other, each of them can be seen as a rare object, which they both, of course, realise and welcome, preparing that "after being perfectly insignificant together they would be decidedly striking apart". This of course, in just a few words prepares us for what is to come.

They are also symmetrical in their attitudes towards each other. "The mother had wished to prevent the father from, as she said, "so much as looking" at the child; the father's plea was that the mother's lightest touch was "simply contamination." At this point we remember the striking image only few lines before "a deep little porcelain cup in which biting acids could be mixed" – Maisie who is to be used as a shuttle between the two parents, a "ready vessel for bitterness.... It was indeed a great deal to be able to say for Ida that no one but Beale desired her blood, and for

Beale that if he should ever have his eyes scratched out it would be only by his wife". The equally match each other's hatred, and therefore are capable equally to inflict great damage. But, on the other hand, as we notice this perfect symmetry we also realize that this is what can prevent the damage they can both do to Maisie, because, as their powers are balanced so will be their influence, their contradicting views will neutralize each other, Of course, this can also create bitterness in Maisie who will grow up learning not to believe either of her parents.

"Poor little monkey!" – exclaims the "good lady" who made an offer to take Maisie, who is to be shared between the two parents, into her care (she must fail of course, because Ida wants to use Maisie as her weapon." "Pray, then, am I to do nothing to counteract his villainous abuse of me?), and this odd expression sticks in our mind and will probably stay there throughout the novel: James himself presents the words as "an epitaph for the tomb of Maisie's childhood". This, second phrase, with a tone of pathos in it gives the dramatic effect to the theme of Maisie's future, which is an undercurrent to the opening chapter. The chapter seems to concentrate on the adults, yet it is Maisie who gets our attention and arouses our expectations as the heroine of the novel, precisely because she is so apparently ignored. And so, with those strange words, but no knowledge yet of Maisie as a person, we wait for her own story to develop.

James avoids sentimentality by his ironic tone. Irony here, as in many cases, is used to create a certain detachment, objectivity, the tone is even formal, the way in which the events are related manages to pack all the information into four pages, again by his use of irony – he puts most of the meaning between the lines. Thus, when the father is unable to render the sum, put down by his wife, as she called it, "in the interest of the child's maintenance", it is up to us to imagine how this sum could have been spent and whether it indeed was originally intended for Maisie. It is up to us, again, to guess about the society "in which for the most part people were occupied only with chatter", and all the dirty sides of it which are not directly exposed to us. And so the other factor is that the opening chapter introduces us to Henry James's style, and from this chapter you learn to understand it and prepare to read it carefully and read between the lines.

Polina Bakhnova, a year thirteen student

Appendix 1

SYLVIA PLATH: DADDY

Daddy

You do not do, you do not do
Any more, black shoe
In which I have lived like a foot
For thirty years, poor and white,
Barely daring to breathe or Achoo.

Daddy, I have had to kill you.
You died before I had time –
Marble-heavy, a bag full of God,
Ghastly statue with one great toe
Big as a Frisco seal

And a head in the freakish Atlantic
Where it pours bean green over blue
In the waters off beautiful Nauset.
I used to pray to recover you.
Ach, du.

In the German tongue, in the Polish town
Scraped flat by the roller
Of wars, wars, wars.
But the name of the town is common.
My Polack friend

Says there are a dozen or two.
So I never could tell where you
Put your foot, your root,
I never could talk to you.
The tongue stuck in my jaw.

It stuck in a barb wire snare.
Ich ich, ich, ich,
I could hardly speak.
I thought every German was you.
And the language obscene.

An engine, an engine
Chuffing me off like a Jew.
A Jew to Dachau, Auschwitz, Belsen.
I began to talk like a Jew.
I think I may well be a Jew.

The snows of the Tyrol, the clear beer of Vienna
Are not very pure or true.
With my gipsy ancestress and my weird luck
And my Taroc pack and my Taroc pack
I may be a bit of a Jew.

I have always been scared of *you*,
With your Luftwaffe, your gobbledygoo.
And your neat mustache
And your Aryan eye, bright blue.
Panzer-man, panzer man, O You –

Not God but a swastika
So black no sky could squeak through.
Every woman adores a Fascist,
The boot in the face, the brute
Brute heart of a brute like you.

You stand at the blackboard, daddy,
In the picture I have of you,
A cleft in your chin instead of your foot
But no less a devil for that, no not
Any less the black man who

Bit my pretty red heart in two.
I was ten when they buried you.
At twenty I tried to die
And get back, back, back to you.
I thought even the bones would do.

But they pulled me out of the sack,
And they stuck me together with glue.
And then I knew what to do.
I made a model of you,
A man in black with a Meinkampf look

And a love of the rack and the screw.
And I said I do, I do.
So daddy, I'm finally through.
The black telephone's off at the root,
The voices just can't worm through.

If I've killed one man, I've killed two—
The vampire who said he was you
And drank my blood for a year,
Seven years, if you want to know.
Daddy, you can lie back now.

There's a stake in your fat black heart
And the villagers never liked you.
They are dancing and stamping on you.
They always *knew* it was you.
Daddy, daddy, you bastard, I'm through.

Appendix 2

CRITICAL TERMINOLOGY

It's always better to use your own words to describe the effects and features of a work of literature than to use technical terms imprecisely or unnecessarily. For most students taking A level English, what matters is understanding what happens in a text, becoming thoroughly familiar with the way it uses language and developing a personal response to it. It is not necessary to dissect and label the parts as if it were a piece of machinery.

If you study literature at university, you'll need to be aware of what the terms used in literary criticism mean. In this appendix you will find some elementary definitions of a few literary terms you may come across or sometimes wish to use. Rather than discuss briefly all the terms you may encounter, we've decided to discuss at some length the ones our students have found the most useful and/or the most tricky to understand.

Alliteration

This is a sound effect where the repetition of initial consonants makes the words more intense, gives them greater emphasis.

> In a **s**ummer **s**eason when **s**oft was the **s**un
> (Langland, *fourteenth century*)

> **B**ent double like old **b**eggars under sacks
> **Kn**ock-**kn**eed, **c**oughing like hags.
> We **c**ursed...
> (Owen, *twentieth century*)

Alliteration has been used in poetry since the earliest times. Repeating soft consonants, as in the Langland example above, produces a gentle, musical sound. Repeating harsh sounds, as in the Owen fragment, produces an ugly, harsh noise.

Ambiguity

If something is ambiguous, it has more than one meaning. For example if someone says, "What a dull day!", the word "dull" could mean "dreary", "overcast", "tedious" or all three. Here the word "dull" is ambiguous.

Poets are particularly fond of conveying two or three ideas simultaneously by deliberately using a word which has a number of meanings. What do you think Hopkins could mean by the word "pitch" when he describes himself as "pitched past pitch of grief"? Or Macbeth mean when he says "So fair and foul a day I have not seen"? In this case "fair" and "foul" could each be understood in several ways.

Sometimes the word "polysemy" is used to describe the same thing.

Assonance

This is a sound effect made by repeating vowel sounds. Written English vowels can have many different sounds (e.g. apple, fast, bathing) so you need to *listen* for this effect, you can't spot it with your eyes.

> With blackest moss the flower-plots
> Were thickly crusted, one and all:
> The rusted nails fell from the knots
> That held the peach to the garden-wall.
> (Tennyson, *nineteenth century*)

> Viciousness in the kitchen!
> The potatoes hiss.
> (Plath, *twentieth century*)

As with alliteration, assonance can intensify gentle or harsh effects.

Quite often a poet will use alliteration and assonance in the same lines to produce richly musical sounds:

> Hard as hurdle arms, with a broth of goldish flue
> Breathed round; the rack of ribs; the scooped flank; lank
> Rope-over thigh; knee-nave; and barrelled shank—
> Head and foot, shoulder and shank
> (Hopkins, *nineteenth century*)

Audience

This is an important concept in literary criticism. The way you write something is conditioned by whom you're writing for. You would probably not use the same kind of language to send even the same message to your father, to your lover, to your neighbour, to your teacher, to your priest or to your dog.

When discussing a text, you need to think about whom the piece was written for and how the writer assumed his or her audience would respond. The most obvious sense in which you need to consider the audience is when you are writing about an extract from a play. How would this work on a theatre audience's thoughts and feelings? But newspapers, poems, letters and even diary entries have audiences too. Ask yourself not just "What is being said here?" but also "Who is it being said to? How does that affect the tone, register, diction, and form in which it is being said?"

Author

Until recently, the term "author" was used to identify the person who wrote a work. So, Charlotte Bronte was called the "author" of the novel *Jane Eyre*. Some critics now prefer to call Charlotte Bronte the "writer" of that novel. This is because the word "author" suggests that what is written is "authorised" or is correct. However, the values embodied in any work don't just depend on the writer. They reflect the religious and social values, the notions of right and wrong, the roles of men and women, the norms of the society in which the writer lived. If certain values or attitudes are "authorised" by a text, that may mean that other values and attitudes could be presented as mad, alien or wrong. But, as we all know, cultures vary, develop and change. Readers brought up in a culture different from the one in which a text was "authorised" may find themselves disagreeing with some of the ideas the work presents as "correct". Many readers may dislike, for example, the way relationships between men and women are presented in *Jane Eyre* or the assumptions that are made in the novel about relationships between people of different social classes. Because what Charlotte Bronte wrote was a reflection of the world in which she grew up not just an expression of her private view of those things it may be advisable to describe her as the "writer" rather than as the "author" of that novel.

Character

In most works of fiction you will come across characters. There are various ways in which you can respond to a character. You may respond as if he or she was someone you know in real life. Often you may identify with a character, wondering how you would behave in similar circumstances, trying to "make sense" of his or her behaviour in psychological terms and trying to imagine how he or she might behave in different circumstances.

But another way of looking at characters in a text is to see them as embodiments of certain values and attitudes, or as representatives of particular cultures. For example, you could see Hamlet as a young man in the midst of family turmoil, which any young man could find himself in today, or instead as an embodiment of certain early seventeenth century, educated, male, London attitudes and concerns: seeing him less as a person about whose inner life you might speculate, more as a collection of cultural attitudes with which you might wish to take issue.

One of the conventions of characterisation is that the outer self – the face, the body, the walk, the clothes—and where the person lives, are strong indicators of the inner self. Do you think this is just a literary convention or is it true in real life? Does the way people you know look tell you a great deal about their personalities? Could a stranger tell much about you by visiting your room?

Most writers use physical description to a greater or lesser extent as a kind of shorthand, a device of economy. We have only to "see" these characters to know quite a lot about them.

> ...there was his son a young squire
> A lover and a lusty bachelor
> With locks curled as they'd been laid in a press
> Of twenty years of age he was I guess
> Of his stature he was of even length
> And wonderfully agile and of great strength
> Embroidered he was, just like a meadow
> All full of fresh flowers, white and red...
> (Chaucer, *fourteenth century*)

> He was a strongly built, rather heavy man of forty, His head was thrust forward, sunk a little between powerful shoulders, and the strong jaw was pushed out aggressively. But the eyes were smouldering, the face hung slack and sodden with drink.
> (Lawrence, *twentieth century*)

When this process is carried further, so that the character's appearance (and behaviour) is simplified, exaggerated and made ridiculous or grotesque, we have what is called a caricature (note the spelling), rather like the puppets you see on "Spitting Image":

> A big, loud man, with a stare and a metallic laugh. A man made out of a coarse material, which seemed to have been stretched out to make so much of him. A man with a great puffed head and forehead, swelled veins in his temples, and such a strained skin to his face that it seemed to hold his eyes open and lift his eyebrows up. A man with a pervading appearance on him of being inflated like a balloon, and ready to start.
>
> (Dickens. *nineteenth century*)

Class

Sociologists see communities as made up of different and competing classes. Some critics argue that texts should be examined for the way they endorse or challenge the assumptions of the richest and/or most powerful classes in society.

Other critics argue that literature stresses individual responsibility, that no matter how powerful social structures and expectations are, moral choices are always the responsibility and are under the control of the individual.

Looking at the way Shakespeare's women characters behave in testing situations might help you to decide to what extent the writer and we see his or her characters as at the mercy of the social structures in which they are presented or as individuals capable of challenging and overcoming them.

For example, here is Ophelia in conversation with her father, Polonius. Knowing the ways that other Shakespearean women challenge their father's authority, for example, in *King Lear*, in *Othello* and in *Romeo and Juliet* may help you to decide how to "read" Ophelia's behaviour here:

POLONIUS: Come your ways
OPHELIA: I shall obey, my lord.

Diction

This is the term used to describe the kinds of words a writer uses in a
particular piece.

Here is someone using colloquial, person-in-the-street diction:

> Wind forever playing loverboy
> bringing he breeze joy
> to everything he touch
> but Wind you can't trust
>
> Forever playing fresh
> with big woman like me...
>   (Agard, *twentieth century*)

In contrast, the diction here is formal, ceremonial and religious:

> Dearly beloved, we are gathered here in the sight of God, and in
> the face of this congregation, to join together this Man and this
> Woman in holy matrimony; which is an honourable estate.
>   (*Book of Common Prayer, sixteenth century*)

Sometimes diction can be described as academic or scientific:

> The addition of the reciprocal operation to the subject's repertory in
> solving scientific problems brings a general advance in strategy and
> tactics: it disposes the subject towards the controlled experiment, that
> is, the nullification of one variable, not simply to study that one vari-
> able, but to study the action of some other variable free from error
> variance contributed by the first.
>   (Flavell, *twentieth century*)

or Romantic:

> A savage place! as holy and enchanted
> As e'er beneath a waning moon was haunted
> By woman's wailing for her demon-lover!
> And from this chasm, with ceaseless turmoil seething,
> As if this Earth in fast thick pants were breathing
> A mighty fountain momently was forced:
> Amidst whose swift half-intermitted burst
> Huge fragments vaulted like rebounding hail...
>   (Coleridge, *nineteenth century*)

The effect of a piece often also depends on the syntax which weaves
the words together. The term "syntax" is explained below.

Figurative Language

One of the features of literary language is the large number of similes and metaphors it uses. Using words *figuratively* is the opposite of using them *literally*. If I write: "Dad was so furious, he was literally climbing up the wall", I am, strictly speaking, talking nonsense. Unless my father has developed suction feet he can't *literally* be climbing up the wall. What I want to say is that he is so angry and agitated that he looks as if he might walk up it. I am describing his behaviour *metaphorically* or *figuratively*.

A simile (notice the spelling) looks like this:

> the rains gather
> like diamonds
> in the fleece of their hair
>   (Grace Nichols, twentieth century)

A metaphor leaves out the "as...as", "than" or "like" to produce something more compact:

> Full of scorpions is my mind, dear wife!
>   (Shakespeare, *seventeenth century*)

If Macbeth had said "I feel as if my mind was full of scorpions" he would have been using a simile. The effect would have been less intense, less horrifying.

Both metaphors and similes are ways of describing something by comparing it with some aspect of something else.

> Sometimes we see a cloud that's dragonish...
>   like a bear or lion,
> A towered citadel, a pendant rock
> A forked mountain, or blue promontory
> With trees upon it...
>   (Shakespeare, *seventeenth century*)

> leaves...like ghosts from an enchanter fleeing
>   (Shelley, *nineteenth century*)

> It is all Hollywood.
>   (Plath, *twentieth century*)

Gender

We are born male or female but our environment conditions us to behave in masculine or feminine ways. This results in what are called gender differences.

Feminist criticism is concerned particularly with how Western European culture has assigned an inferior status to women, presenting as "natural" differences between the sexes which have been socially constructed. Many stories assume certain preconceptions about what being "masculine" or "feminine" means. When you write about a text, you may feel that these implicit assumptions are ones which need to be made explicit, commented upon or challenged.

It is as important for male readers to question the notions of masculinity presented in a text, as it is for female readers to challenge what is presented as feminine. Many males would challenge notions of masculinity if these assumed that being masculine involved behaving like a bully (whether to women or to so-called inferiors); always deferring to those in authority in the belief that orders must be obeyed whether they were good or bad, or valuing order and discipline above such qualities as imagination, freedom, love and creativity.

Ideology

This is your whole way of seeing the world. Imagine a line of concentration camp victims. Shorn of their hair, they have lost their families and all their possessions. They have numbers instead of names and their common fate is sealed. One person in the line has absolute faith that God orders all things for the best. The next one believes that everything in the world is decided by economic, political and social conditions and is certain there is no such thing as the soul which survives the body. Another person in the line believes that after death people are reincarnated as animals or plants. The three people share the same planet, will suffer what appears to be common a fate (death in the gas chamber) yet each lives, in a sense, in a completely different universe.

A person's ideology is formed by his or her upbringing, education, faith, imagination, experiences and judgements. It is often worth examining the ideological assumptions which underlie a work of literature. In many works of literature (for example, Dickens's *Hard Times* and Shakespeare's *Antony and Cleopatra*) much of the excitement comes from the tensions which arise when two totally different ideologies come into conflict with each other.

Image and Imagery

An image is a picture in words:

> The leaves fluttered in the breeze.

> Tyger! Tyger! burning bright
> In the forests of the night...
>   (Blake, *eighteenth century*)

> into this crazed man-made
> stone brain
>   (Atwood, *twentieth century*)

An image may be a literal representation of something seen, as in the first example, or an imaginative or figurative way of seeing something, as in the second and third examples above.

Many of Shakespeare's plays use groups of images which are peculiar to them. For example, in *Hamlet* there are many images describing blisters, ulcers, tumours, disease and physical corruption. Taken together this imagery gives the language and thoughts of this play a particular tone and colour. We feel there is something "rotten in the state of Denmark".

It's very important not to confuse the words "image" and "impression". Our *impression* of Denmark in *Hamlet* is built up from many different *images*. Similarly, in a literature essay it's less confusing to talk about the *impression* we get of a particular character than about his or her *image*. There will probably be a large number of images which help to form that impression.

Irony

This is a particularly tricky term to define.

We use irony every day when we use a sarcastic tone of voice to show that what we appear to be saying is not what we mean: "Oh fantastic! I've got a Maths examination today followed by two hours' History and then a six-mile cross-country run in a hailstorm! I can hardly contain my delight!..."

Meaning is a matter of words. But looking up definitions in a dictionary is just a starting point. The *tone* and thus the full meaning of words in use cannot be found in a dictionary.

If you looked up these words in a dictionary: hooligan; villain; delinquent; rascal; monster; reprobate, you'd find they have terrible meanings. So why does a four year old laugh when his mother growls and calls him one of these things? It is the tone of voice which is a large part of the meaning of words in use. It's the mother's theatrical tone of voice which signals to the child that she means the very opposite of what she appears to be saying. The child's laughter is a recognition of the mismatch between what's being said and the way it's being said.

Such a mismatch is called irony and is one of the most powerful of the writer's tools. What appears to be said is undercut by the way it is being said and the effect on us depends upon our being able to pick that up. When reading to ourselves it is easy to be led astray by taking words at their face value. Perhaps you've hurt someone by writing them a letter which you intended as a joke and which they took seriously?

Not much literature is deadly solemn. "Boring" may be the word a student uses to describe a passage full of words s/he doesn't understand. But often it signals that s/he has missed the irony. Once the mismatch between the words and the way they are being said is detected, the meaning suddenly becomes plain and the piece funny. For an extended study of passages which make points through their irony see pages 76, 97 and 133. You may like to find W H Auden's poem "The Unknown Citizen" in the library. The poem is ironic from beginning to end.

Metre

The fundamental difference between poetry and prose is that poetry organises words on the page rhythmically.

If we come across a piece of poetry written out as if it were prose we usually feel ourselves picking up the pattern; stressing some syllables and not stressing others. What happens, for example, when you read these lines aloud a few times?

A dungeon horrible, on all sides round, as one great furnace, flamed; yet from those flames no light; but rather darkness visible served only to discover sights of woe, regions of sorrow, doleful shades, where peace and rest can never dwell; hope never comes that comes to all; but torture without end still urges, a fiery deluge, fed with ever-burning sulphur unconsumed.

As you read and reread these lines you will probably begin to feel a regular pulse beating. The words break down naturally into lines in each of which there are five stressed syllables. The pattern is easier to see when we write the piece out as verse:

A **dun**geon **horrible**, on **all** sides **round**,
As **one** great **fur**nace, **flamed**; yet **from** those **flames**
No **light**; but **ra**ther **darkness visible**
Served **only to** dis**cover sight**s of **woe**,
Regions of **sorrow**, **dole**ful **sha**des, where **peace**
And **rest** can **never dwell**; hope **never comes**
That **comes** to **all**; but **tor**ture **without end**
Still **urges**, **by** a **fie**ry **de**luge, **fed**
With **ever-bur**ning **sul**phur **uncon**sumed.
    (Milton, *seventeenth century*)

There are names for different kinds of metre. Because the verse above, like most of Shakespeare's has five stressed syllables in each line, it is called *pentameter*, after the Greek word for five or, more commonly, *heroic metre.*

In this extract, Shakespeare uses a different metre:

When shall **we** three **meet** a**gain**?
In **thun**der, **light**ning **or** in **rain**?
When the **hurlyburly's done**,
When the **bat**tle's **lost** and **won**.
That will **be** ere **set** of **sun**.

In this case each line has four stressed syllables and the metre is known as *tetrameter.*

Stressed syllables have more weight, more emphasis, more importance than unstressed ones. Often it's worth showing how a poet achieves a dramatic effect by looking at where the stresses fall.

O the **mind** has **moun**tains **cliffs** of **fall**
Frightful.

The stress here on the syllable "fright" is particularly disturbing.

In the examples above, you will notice that the final syllable of each line is stressed. This is the case in most English poetry. When we have lines ending with unstressed syllables, the effect can be restless and disturbing:

Who are these? Why sit they here in twi**light**?
Wherefore rock they, purgatorial sha**dows**,
Drooping tongues from jaws that slob their rel**ish**,
Baring teeth that leer like skulls' teeth wick**ed**?
    (Owen, *twentieth century*)

The usual way to show which syllables are stressed and which are not is like this:

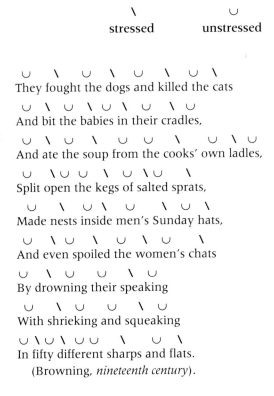

They fought the dogs and killed the cats
And bit the babies in their cradles,
And ate the soup from the cooks' own ladles,
Split open the kegs of salted sprats,
Made nests inside men's Sunday hats,
And even spoiled the women's chats
By drowning their speaking
With shrieking and squeaking
In fifty different sharps and flats.
  (Browning, *nineteenth century*).

Mimesis

This is mimicking either the movement, the shape, the size or the texture of something by using words which suggest it. So when Lawrence describes a snake like this:

> He reached down from a fissure in the earth-wall in the gloom
> And trailed his yellow-brown slackness soft-bellied down, over the
>   edge of the stone trough
> And rested...

the slow, sinuous movement of the words *mimics* the movement of the snake. As we read aloud and feel the rhythm of his words, we get a strong impression of what Lawrence observed.

Here's Shakespeare imitating the rhythm of a galloping horse to give a panicky feel to the action being described:

> Now spurs the lated traveller apace
> To gain the timely inn.

The traveller wants to reach the inn before nightfall—it's dangerous being out alone at night in Macbeth's kingdom!

Similarly the rhythm and movement of Eliot's verse gives us a comical and powerful feeling of activity here:

> The person in the Spanish cape
> Tries to sit on Sweeney's knees
>
> Slips and pulls the table cloth
> Overturns a coffee-cup,
> Reorganised upon the floor
> She yawns and draws a stocking up;

Words can also mimic a sensation, adding power to a simile:

> The fluorescent light wincing on and off like a terrible migraine
>   (Plath: *twentieth century*)

the bulk of something:

> his dreadnought breast and braids of thew
>   (Hopkins: *nineteenth century*)

confusion and panic:

> An ecstasy of fumbling
> Fitting the clumsy helmets
>   (Owen : *twentieth century*)

or, through the texture of the words, emphasise smoothness:

> And smooth as monumental alabaster
>   (Shakespeare: *seventeenth century*)

or roughness:

> The rugged Pyrrus, like th'Hyrcanian beast
>   (Shakespeare: *seventeenth century*)

In all these cases we are being given at the same time *information* from the meaning of the words and a *sensation* produced by the movement, sound or texture of the words.

Onomatopoeia

This mouthful of a word describes a very simple sound-effect. "Crash", "wallop", "thud", "tinkle" "moan" and "squeak" are all examples of it. The sounds of the words imitate the sounds they describe.

> The Bullets chirped—In vain! vain! vain!
> Machine guns chuckled—Tit-tut! Tut-tit!
> And the Big Gun guffawed.
>
> Another sighed...
> And the falling splinters tittered.
>   (Owen: *twentieth century*)

It's important not to confuse *onomatopoeia* (which is the imitation of *sounds*) with *mimesis* which can be the imitation of *movements, weight, texture* or *bulk.*

Personification

This is the trick of describing something that isn't a person as if it were. Animals, trees, rocks, telephones, trains and even dustbins have come in for personification at times. Here's Shakespeare using it to make a scene come alive:

> There is a willow grows aslant a brook
> That shows his hoar leaves in the glassy stream...
> There, on the pendant bows her coronet weeds
> Clambering to hang, an envious sliver broke;
> When down her weedy trophies and herself
> Fell in the weeping brook...
>   But long it could not be
> Till that her garments, heavy with their drink,
> Pulled the poor wretch from her melodious lay
> To muddy death.

Symbol

> Lion-hearted Macbeth
>   (Shakespeare: *seventeenth century*)
>
> Iram indeed is gone with all its Rose
>   (Fitzgerald: *nineteenth century*)

> I'm a fullblooded
> West Indian Stereotype
> See me straw hat?
> Watch it good
> (Agard: *twentieth century*)

In each of these examples, the writer is assuming that the readers will recognise the lion, the rose and the straw hat not simply as the everyday things they are but as symbols for certain qualities, ideas, attitudes to life. The lion has traditionally been a symbol not just of strength and bravery but of royalty. The rose in much European literature symbolises love, the fragility, preciousness and sensual appeal of beauty. The straw hat, Agard implies, is what many whites associate with West Indians: a casual, easy-going attitude to life.

Syntax

Syntax is the grammatical structure of words in a sentence. The most straight-forward way of ordering the following information is:

The cat sat on the mat.

If we change the word order and write:

On the mat, the cat sat *or*

Sat the cat on the mat

the result is less mundane but harder to understand: the syntax is undergoing strain.

And if we radically alter the word-order:

Mat the cat sat on the

we are writing something almost unintelligible because the syntax, the grammatical relationship between the words, is almost impossible to grasp.